Because
I Lived It

Daily Devotions from a life
changed by God's grace

LEIGH ANN MADDING

WESTBOW
PRESS
A DIVISION OF THOMAS NELSON

WestBow Press books may be ordered through booksellers or by contacting:

WestBow Press
A Division of Thomas Nelson
1663 Liberty Drive
Bloomington, IN 47403
www.westbowpress.com
1-(866) 928-1240

Because of the dynamic nature of the Internet, any Web addresses or links contained in this book may have changed since publication and may no longer be valid. The views expressed in this work are solely those of the author and do not necessarily reflect the views of the publisher, and the publisher hereby disclaims any responsibility for them.

ISBN: 978-1-4497-0429-2 (sc)
ISBN: 978-1-4497-0430-8 (hc)
ISBN: 978-1-4497-0484-1 (e)

Library of Congress Control Number: 2010934083

Printed in the United States of America

WestBow Press rev. date: 9/21/2010

Acknowledgements

I would like to thank all of those who have made this journey with me. I have been blessed with such great people in my life. There are a few that I would like to thank personally.

Michael, you are my best friend and have proven that time and time again. You stood by me through the darkness and helped me into the light.

Amy, Lori, and Heather; you three have been the perfect harmony to keep me sane. You have held me up and held me down. I know God chose us, because no one could have chosen better. It is my blessing and priviledge to call each of you "friend."

Dr. David Moore, you have been a great supportor and mentor. You gave me a security in my writing that could have been easily crippled. Thank you so much for being someone I can depend on.

My devotional list friends, you have been more of a blessing to me than I could have ever imagined. I just started sharing some thoughts and struggles with my spiritual walk and growth and learned that I wasn't the only one. I love talking to each one of you and look forward to many more chats!

My friends, each of you have been a support that I cannot imagine being without. I have so many that I have laughed and cried with.

Been silly and been serious with. Grown and matured in Christ with. No one could be more blessed than I am with my friends.

My family, I know I have put all of you through it in the past, but thank you for not giving up on me. I gave you plenty of reason to do just that. I wouldn't be the person I am today without each one of you. I have been blessed with a loving and caring family. I love you very much.

My parents,I dedicate this book to you. You have always been my biggest supporters and I know there have been times when that must have been hard. You have always been Godly examples for me, even when I wasn't paying attention. Please know how much my heart swells when I think of you. I have no idea where I would be today without you. God placed me in your arms many years ago. I just thank Him so much that you never let go!

Most importantly, I would like to thank my Lord and Savior, Jesus Christ! I have experienced true love, mercy, grace and forgiveness. I know there is no life, only existence, without You! I am so thankful that I can never be snatched from Your faithful hands! You have made life truly worth living and my daily prayer is that I show this to you every day!

Introduction

I decided long ago to start writing devotionals and started sending them to family and friends. What I had been encouraged to do was to start journaling, but found that I didn't really like that. So, I guess I considered this my journal, but not one that I keep under lock and key, one that I share with others. I would have never dreamed how my little journal would grow. I now have a list of people, some I don't even know, getting them daily. I even have some who will call me or email me when I'm off work, and ask where their daily devotional is.

I have never claimed to be a great writer or a perfect Christian. I think that maybe why they've been so popular. I'm just an ordinary person, sharing her ordinary thoughts, on an ordinary day. I share my thoughts, my fears, and my questions with those I feel might sometimes feel the same way. I never claim to have the answers, but I can travel this road called life with you. Together, we can struggle through, then dance together in heaven, where there will be no more tears, no more struggle, and no more confusion – just an eternity in paradise, praising our Lord and Savior forever more!

I have shared in my devotionals that I'm not perfect, but have never shared my testimony. I will share a little of it now.

I was saved at the age of 8 and by the age of 30 I felt my life was beyond help, that I had fallen too far off the path, that God wouldn't want anything to do with someone like me.

I do believe I was saved and I don't believe you can lose your salvation, so where does that leave a person like me? It leaves a person with a weak faith.

As a child, teenager, and young adult, I was under the assumption that believing was enough. I believed in Jesus. I believed He died on the cross for my sins. I believed that if I asked Him, He would come into my heart. I did that. I prayed that prayer. I believed every word I said. What I have now realized is that belief and faith are two very different things. Belief and dependence are two very different things. I had always believed in God, but I had never depended on Him.

Growing up in a small southern town, church was something I was expected to do. It wasn't, "Do you go to church?" it was "What church do you go to?" That is just what we did. I have gone to church my whole life. I did missions, Bible school, choir, youth group. I was there every time the doors were opened. So what was I missing? I was missing the "why." Why was I doing all these things? Why was I there every time the doors were opened? Even though growing up in church is a blessing, you need to be careful not to let it become a habit instead of a faith. Just because you have sung "Jesus loves me" a thousand times, and have memorized scripture in Sunday School (usually starting with John 3:16), doesn't mean that you automatically have what it takes to fight temptation. It doesn't mean you have a strong faith.

It only takes one bad decision to take you down that path I followed. One bad decision usually leads to another. It can be a domino effect after that. I think my biggest mistake was assuming my faith was strong. I truly thought it was. I was saved, what else is there to do? What I have now realized is that if you have a weak faith, you have weak defenses. I wasn't strong enough to fight any temptation that came my way.

When I decided to seek help, a counselor told me was that I needed to work on my spiritual life. I laughed. Then with great arrogance, I preceded to tell her that I sang solos in my church, and that my church was on TV. People knew me at my church – that's how much

I was there! Then, it was her turn to laugh. She said, "Leigh Ann, I didn't ask about your church attendance. I asked about your faith." I was baffled. I had never distinguished between the two. It was all the same, wasn't it? No, I found out that it isn't. I went to church. I had a routine. I had a habit. I did what I was told. I believed what I was told. I had my father's faith. I had my mother's faith. I didn't have a faith of my own. I didn't have a relationship with God. I was a hypocrite.

I used to be the kind of "self-professed" Christian that Satan loves. I told everyone I was a Christian. I did sing for my church on TV. I "talked the talk," but didn't "walk the walk." I shutter every time I think about the witness opportunities I destroyed. How many people did I influence the wrong way? Once, while I was still in the midst of my chaos, our pastor said something in a sermon I will never forget. I couldn't tell you what the topic of the sermon was that day, but his words cut right through me. At the time, I just thought it was amazing that I was listening. Now, I know that this was once of the times (and there were many), that God was trying to get my attention. But he asked the congregation, "Are you an example or an excuse?" I felt like he was speaking right to me. Have you ever had a moment in church where you feel like the preacher, the sound man, and the light man all got together to gang up on you? Well, this was one of those moments for me. I felt like the preacher's voice got louder and a spot light was shining right on me! I was no example for anyone. Not a good one anyway. I was an excuse for all who knew me. Why would my life help those to come to Jesus? "She's no different than me," I'm sure they would say or "Look at her singing, if they had only seen her last night!" I was a tool for Satan, an excuse for all around.

The turning point for me was one night I was taken by a lake in Jackson, Mississippi. For those who know me, you know I'm not much of a nature lover, so this is even more strange. As I walked over to the water, I noticed the moon shining across the water. I was struck with how beautiful it was and I started to cry. My friends left me. I think they somehow knew something big and very private was happening to me. I started to cry, not because of the beauty before me, but because I couldn't remember the last time I thought something was beautiful that money had not bought, or that man had not made. God had put so much beauty in the world, and I had stopped noticing it. I had stopped noticing Him. I dropped to my knees right there beside that lake and through my tears, I asked God to forgive me. I said, "Okay God. You have been trying to get my attention for a while now. I'm so sorry I ignored you. Here you go. Now, right now, I give my life to you. I've made a mess of it and what's left isn't much, but it's yours. Please take it, I have proven that I can't do this on my own. I need you and I'm sorry."

That was many years ago, and I have never looked back on that life. I don't miss any part of it. I thought my life was over. I have learned that is when it began. Do I have regrets? Sure. Do I have resentments? No. I have prayed that God use my past for His purpose. I have prayed that He use my experience to reach out to others. I have prayed this prayer and He gave me you. My prayer is that each of you take something from my story. If you are on the right road, stay on it. Taking a detour isn't worth it! Find your faith and make it strong. If you are already on the wrong road, just turn around. It's never too late and I don't believe in lost causes. One of my favorite quotes says, "just as a story cannot truly be told unless you tell it from beginning to end, a life cannot be judged from somewhere in the middle." Your past doesn't define you. Your present can be changed. And your future is up to you. Find your faith and make it strong. Make good choices. Let God lead you. Don't end up like me and have to hand God the wreckage of your life and say, "Okay God. You have been trying to get my attention for a while now. I'm so sorry I ignored you. Here you go. Now, right now, I give my life to you. I've made a mess of it and what's left isn't much, but it's yours. Please take it, I have proven that I can't do this on my own. I need you and I'm sorry." Give your life to Him before He has to put you back together. Give you life to Him before you make those first bad decisions. Give your life to Him and be an example, not an excuse. Don't just believe, have faith!

His blessings to you all,

Leigh Ann Madding

January 1

Eternal Life

Therefore, if anyone is in Christ, he is a new creation;
old things have passed away; behold, all things
have become new.- 2 Corinthians 5:17

At this time of year, we say goodbye to the previous year and welcome in the new. Hopefully, we don't regret our past, but have learned from it. Hopefully, we have built memories.

Life on earth consists of the good and the bad, happy and sorrowful events, contented and frustrated people. We can now look to the new near with joyful anticipation at what might come next.

The new year can remind us of the new creation we are in Christ. The old self is replaced by a new and eternal "self" we can enjoy and cultivate. This life, like last year, will pass away, but our life with Jesus is eternal!

January 2

Who Changed?

I am the Lord, I do not change. – Malachi 3:6

In a world where you can barely keep up with change, we have one promised constant, and that is Jesus. Not only is our world ever changing, but we are as well. Have you ever stopped to examine how many people you are everyday? Are you one person at work? One with your family? One with your friends? One around people you don't know? One at church? Sometimes, I feel like we should all receive Oscars for all the acting we do, for all the different roles that we play. I know I should have won a few in my lifetime.

Isn't it wonderful to know that our God does not change? He is always the same. He always loves us. He is always faithful. He is always wise. He is always there. He always wants what is best for us. If you don't feel as close to God as you use to, who do you think changed? If you have never felt as close to God as you should or want to, who do you think needs to change? Pray today that your "promised constant" in Jesus shows in all the different roles you play in your daily life!

January 3

Staying Charged

Let your light shine before men, that they may see your good
deeds and praise your Father in heaven. – Matthew 5:16

Have you ever tried to use a flashlight and found that the batteries were dead? You can't see the path ahead with a flashlight whose batteries are out of juice. You can buy rechargeable batteries that plug into a power source when not in use so they are fully charged the next time they are needed.

During Jesus' life on earth, He knew the necessity of recharging. Scripture tells us, "So He often withdrew into the wilderness and prayed" (Luke 5:16). We aren't any different. We need to recharge our batteries too. We need to plug ourselves into our Power Source daily in order to stay charged for those times we will need it. Plug into Jesus. Through Him, get the strength you need for whatever may come your way. Make sure your inner flashlight is never out of juice so people will see His light shine through you!

Simple Instructions

And what does the Lord require of you? To act justly and to love mercy and to walk humbly with your God. – Micah 6:8

Our pastor once used this verse in his sermon, and it got me thinking. So many people out there wonder, "What does God want with me?" and "What am I supposed to be doing?" Some who do the asking, never go looking for the answers. Scripture is full of guidance and instruction. It's full of promise and prophecy. If you want to know what you should be doing, the Scriptures are a good place to start.

Paul tells us to "rejoice always, to pray without ceasing and in everything give thanks" (1 Thessalonians 5:16-18). James tells us to "humble ourselves before God" (James 4:7). Deuteronomy says, "love the Lord with all your heart, soul, mind and strength" (Deuteronomy 6:5). Micah 6:8 reads "act justly, love mercy, and walk humbly." The answer to the questions "What does God want with me?" and "What am I supposed to be doing?" couldn't be written any simpler or more clearly than that!

I have given you just a few passages of Scripture to answer those questions. There are many, many more. "God is not the author of confusion" (1 Corinthians 14:33). He loves you and wants you to know His will for your life. Although I never feel like I'm perfect, I have found that if I talk to Him, study His word, and try to live by my faith; I feel close to Him and His will for my life!

ぉや やぉ

January 5

Questions Answered

God does great things which we cannot comprehend. – Job 37:5

I don't know about you, but I struggle a lot with understanding. Why does God love someone like me? Why, with everything going on in this world, would He bother with my request? What about me is so special? Then, I go to the more generic questions – Why do good things happen to bad people and bad things happen to good people? Why do children die? Why does cancer exist? Why.....? Why.....? Why.....?

In the end, I must accept that God's grace is sufficient, that He loves me, that His will is perfect and that He is God! I have to accept that there are things in life that don't make sense I have to trust that "all thing work for the good of those who love God" (Romans 8:28). He knows everything and I only know a fraction. The big picture is not within my little world.

We have an amazing God who does amazing things, both things we see, and things we are blind to, things we will understand, and things we won't, things we accept, and things we can't seem to. I'm reminded of the verse, "For we walk by faith, and not by sight" (2 Corinthians 5:7). Without faith, this world can seem disproportionate. Without faith, this world will never make sense. Without faith, your questions will never find answers!

January 6

Your Days are Numbered

Teach us to number our days and recognize how few they are; help us to spend them as we should. – Psalm 90:12

Have you ever had someone ask you, "What would you do if you knew that you were going to die tomorrow….or in six months….or in a year?" I think we have all played this "what if?" game. People will answer with things like, "I'd go and see the world," "I'd quit working and enjoy life," or "I'd spend all my time with my family." Have you ever had anyone say, "Well, I'd tell as many people as I could about Jesus!"?

We are all dying in a literal sense. From birth, each day that passes gets us closer to our death. That may sound morbid, but it's still true. What are you doing with your time? What are your activities? What do you talk about? What are your goals? This prayer in Psalms is one we should say each morning, "Help me to spend this day as I should." In other words, "God, what do you want from me today?"

Should I Expect Miracles?

What good is it, my brothers, if a man claims to have faith but has no deeds? Can such faith save him? – James 2:14

One time, as I was listening to a church service on television. The pastor said something that I had to stop and write down. He said, "It's foolish to think that God will give you miracles, when you are walking in disobedience." Wow!

Many people profess to have faith in Jesus. Many profess to be Christians. Can you tell by their lifestyles that they are telling the truth? Can others see that truth in you? Stating that you are a Christian and living like one are, unfortunately, sometimes two completely different things! How many of us fall into the category "talk the talk, but don't walk the walk"?

Search your heart and life today and then answer this question for yourself: "Should I expect miracles?"

January 8

Planning Right

We can make our own plans, but the Lord gives
the right answer. – Proverbs 16:1

We all make plans. We make small plans everyday. "What am I going to do on Friday night?" "Do I cook dinner or do I order out?" "Should I rent a movie or is there something good on TV?" "Do I really need that cookie?" We also make big plans about things like marriage, family, career, and retirement. We tend to think our plans are good. They're what's best for us. After all, people don't usually set themselves up for failure and mistakes!

We might know that we need to seek God's help with the big stuff and hopefully we seek it. But, some may wonder, "Do I really need to seek His help for my Friday night plans?" Well, that depends on what you normally do on a Friday night. The small decisions are important too! A small mistake can cause big problems! Seek God's guidance. Pray about your decisions. Don't make hasty choices. When mistakes happen, don't add to them and make things worse. We do have the free will to make our own plans; we just need to make sure God is a big part of carrying them out!

January 9

Patient Endurance

Patient endurance is what you need now, so that you
will continue to do God's will. Then you will receive
all that was promised. – Hebrews 10:36

A friend of mine sent me this verse. He couldn't have known, but God knew that I needed patient endurance that very day. We all need patient endurance to run the race of life. We already know where the finish line is, we just don't know how long our leg of the race will be.

When you feel like you can't take anymore, look to God for strength. When you feel like a prayer will never be answered, look to God for patience and peace. When you feel like you have no idea what to do next, look to God for a light to show the way. Paul said, "I have fought the good fight, I have finished the race, I have kept the faith" (2 Timothy 4:7). My prayer is that one day, I will be able to say the same!

꧁꧂

Asking for Help

Consider this: You do not support the root, but
the root supports you. – Romans 11:18

Every year when Christmas is over, I put all of my decorations back into their storage containers. Once, instead of asking someone to help me put them away, I just decided to do it myself thinking it would be quicker and on my time schedule. I don't always like to depend on others and I know this is arrogant and impatient thinking. While lifting my Christmas tree box up over my head, having one foot on my washer and the other on my dryer, I heard my back pop. Moral of the story? I could have saved myself a few weeks of pain by just asking for help.

We tend to think that we can do everything on our own, even when it comes to our faith. We often say, "God, I've got this one. I'll call you if I need you!" Faith can only be as strong as the strength of what your faith is in. Is your faith in yourself, or is it in Jesus? Isaiah 40:31 says, "But those who wait on the Lord shall renew their strength; they shall mount on wings like eagles, they shall run and not be weary, they shall walk and not faint." Don't wait until you hurt yourself, ask Jesus to help you today!

Making Time to Pray

He departed to the mountain to pray. – Mark 6:46

Jesus had a pretty hectic schedule, but He always found time for prayer. He spent His days giving, preaching, healing and being followed by a mob of people (and not always a friendly mob). He knew that it was important to spend time with His Father. He not only loved His father and wanted to spend time with Him, but He also needed to be replenished and renewed in Him.

Just as our cars cannot run forever on fumes, neither can we. We need to make the time to stop and spend some time getting "refueled" by the Holy Spirit. We get tired and spent. This world is a very demanding place to be. Always make time for prayer! The Bible tells us to "go into your room, and when you have shut your door, pray to your Father" (Matthew 6:6). Spending time with God keeps us filled with the Spirit and keeps us focused on what's important. Getting replenished and renewed with the Spirit makes our demanding world and hectic schedules easier to bear!

Loving the Flawed

Love keeps no record of wrongs. – 1 Corinthians 13:5

We have all done things we regret. We have those closest to us won't let us forget it. We also have those who make us feel that their love goes beyond what we think we might deserve. God's love for us is stronger than anything we have done. He loves us so much that when we come to Him for forgiveness, it's given, then it's done and we can move on.

Showing God's love and acceptance for others can save someone's life, both physically and spiritually. Showing mercy and compassion for a fallen child of God can bring them back to Him. Showing the ability to forgive and not bring it up again, can make someone see Him in you. Let's not keep a tally of wrongs. Just as God does for us, let's love in spite of flaws, both our own and in others.

ﻬﻬ

January 13

Looking Back

The thief does not come except to steal, and to kill, and
to destroy. I have come that they may have life, and that
they may have it more abundantly. – John 10:10

Have you ever tried to drive your car while looking out of the back
window? Have you ever thought about why the rear view mirror is
so small and the front windshield takes up most of your line of sight?
Maybe the reason is that it's more important to look forward than to
look back. Many people waste so much of their time and energy with
guilt from past mistakes or failures, reliving old glories, or missing
a time or love lost. We think about what has slipped through our
fingers, instead of holding on to what is in the here and now.

We should be focused on our present and our future. We should
be trying to fulfill God's will in our lives and live abundantly. If
we missed out on a past purpose, God has a new one ready to go.
Don't let Satan steal your future by using your past as a weapon.
Just glance in your rear view mirror every once in a while to smile
at past blessings, remember lessons learned, and then move on to
your future!

〜

January 14

Help My Unbelief

Immediately the father of the child cried out and said with
tears, "Lord, I believe; help my unbelief!" – Mark 9:24

When I read this verse, I could completely understand where this
man was coming from. How many times have I said I believe in
Jesus, and not just that He was here and real, but in all of Him?
How many times have I said I trust Him, only to still do things my
own way? How many times have I said that I loved Him, only to do
things that I know hurt Him? How many times have I said that I
believe in His promises, that He will take care of me, and that all I
need is Him, only to find myself doubting and wanting?

Many of us are afraid to go to Jesus with a request like this man had.
We are afraid to express out loud that we believe, but we don't. Jesus
knows our hearts. I think saying to Him, "Lord, I believe; help my
unbelief" is something He'd like to hear and help you with.

January 15

Giving to the Poor

Being kind to the poor is like lending to the Lord; He will
reward you for what you have done. – Proverbs 19:17

When I read this passage, I thought of giving to the food pantry
or serving meals at a homeless shelter. Both of these are wonderful,
selfless acts that need to be done and benefit many. But, this isn't the
only kind of poor. Yes, there are the financially poor, but there are
also the spiritually poor. Someone can have everything this world
has to offer and be the poorest person we know. We need to give of
ourselves to these poor souls as well.

A kind word spoken at the right moment, a hug given just because,
compassion and mercy to the down hearted, the gospel shared with
a lost stranger ; all of these things can be a service given to the poor,
the spiritually poor. Jesus said, "The poor you will always have with
you, and you can help them any time you want" (Mark 14:7). Is that
time now? What will you give to the poor today?

January 16

Keep Your Promise

And she made a vow, saying, "O Lord Almighty, if you will only look upon your servant's misery and remember me." – 1 Samuel 1:11

Hannah was a woman who desperately longed for a child. She was miserable because she was barren. She prayed to the Lord and promised that if He gave her a child, she in return would give the child back to the Lord and His service. After praying this prayer, she replied, "May your servant find favor in Your eyes" (1 Samuel 1:18) – and favor was given. She had a son and named him Samuel, saying, "Because I asked the Lord for him" (1 Samuel 1:20). As she promised, when Samuel was old enough, she gave him up. She left him with Eli, the priest, so he could grow up to serve the Lord. This couldn't have been easy for her. I'm sure her selfish side wanted to forget the promise she had made to the Lord and kept her son. But, because of the promise she kept, the Lord blessed her with three more sons and two daughters.

Have you ever said, "God if you do this for me, then I promise to ...."? Have you followed through? Many times, we can get so wrapped up in what we want, that nothing else matters. Then, once we get it, again, nothing else matters. We tend to forget everything else. When we make promises to God, we should think of Hannah. She followed through with her promise and was continually blessed. Sometimes what we are giving up opens the door to so much more. Don't use promises to God as a bargaining tool. Take them seriously and follow through. He always keeps His promises, shouldn't we do the same?

Before You Ask

For your Father knows the things you have need
of before you ask Him. – Matthew 6:8

Why do we have to ask God for something if He already knows what we want? Why doesn't He just go ahead and do it? To be honest with you, I have asked myself these very questions and the answer I have found is a "relationship". God is waiting for you to build a relationship with Him and this relationship starts with trusting Him with your requests. It grows when you communicate with Him about your life. Then it builds into something that is not just a list of things you need, but a friendship that is precious.

When you find yourself thinking, "Why ask?" examine your relationship with God. Are you talking to Him about things other that your want, needs, or problems? Are you seeking His will and His way? He does know what you want, but He is just waiting for you to come and share it with Him. He wants to have a relationship with you. He wants to be a part of your life, not just a solution to your problems!

ᴈᴖᴑ ᴑᴑᴈᴖ

January 18

Don't Lie

And the Lord said to Cain, "Where is Abel your brother?" Cain said, "I do not know. Am I my brother's keeper?" – Genesis 4:9

When I was little, and I had done something wrong, my parents would give me an opportunity to confess what I had done before they would admit they already new. When I cut my own hair, when I overflowed the bathroom sink, when I put a big "X marks Papa's spot" on one of my grandmother's dinning room chairs, my parents knew I was the culprit. The reason they would ask me about it was to see if I would tell the truth.

Just as God knew Cain had murdered his brother Abel, God knows what we have done. He just wants us to be honest with Him. It may not be as severe as murder, but we have all sinned against God. All He wants is for us to confess with our mouths and repent in our hearts. He doesn't want us to lie, shift blame, or avoid. He wants us to come to Him and talk to Him about it. Lying about what we have done seems a little silly when He already knows. All we do is dig ourselves in deeper. I knew that lying to my father always made things worse and that holds true with my Heavenly Father as well!

Willing Servant

Be shepherds of God's flock that is under your care,
serving as overseers – not because you must, but
because you are willing, as God wants you to be; not
greedy for money, but eager to serve. – 1 Peter 5:2

When I read this verse, I was struck by its simple and honest words, "not because you must, but because you are willing". Obligation verses obedience is where I sometimes struggle. Growing up, I thought you "had" to do this, or you "had" to do that. To be honest, thinking that I had to do it, often made me not want to do it. As an adult, I have come to know the difference between the two. I don't sing in the choir because I have to. I don't work with the youth out of obligation. I don't write devotionals because I think I'm good at it. I do these things because I feel like this is where God want me to be and what He wants me to be doing. I am willing to serve where I can.

We are called to be servants of God's will. We are called to help His children. We are called to spread His Word. Jesus said of Himself, "I did not come to be served, but to serve" (Matthew 20:28). If you can change your thinking from "I have to do this" to "I am willing to do what I can", I can tell you that based on my own experience you will be blessed by the difference!

January 20

Out of the Valley

I will restore to you the years that the swarming
locust has eaten. – Joel 2:25

If any of you are like me, you have a period in your life that wasn't easy. Whether it was your fault or accidental circumstances, there might have been a time when you felt as though "you were walking through the valley" (Psalm 23). These dark valleys in life can make us lose our way, they can make us bitter, and they can cause us to lose our faith. Don't let this happen to you! Come to Jesus and He will help you find your way out, into a life abundant (John 10:10).

Letting Jesus into your heart and into these moments of despair can change your life. You can learn to lean on Him and can learn that you don't have to go through anything alone. You can learn that "all things work together for the good to those who love God" (Romans 8:28). Now, when I look back on my dark times, I know that physically, I'm not able to get those years back, but through Jesus, they can mean something completely different. I know it was Him that brought me out of my dark valley and into the light!

January 21

Childhood Beliefs

When I was a child, I spoke as a child, I understood as
a child, I thought as a child; but when I became a man,
I put away childish things. - 1 Corinthians 13:11

When I was a child, I believed in Santa Claus, the Easter Bunny, my father was the strongest man in the world, and a kiss from my mother made everything better. As a child, I believed in and trusted in many things. Included in these beliefs was Jesus. Now, I no longer believe in Santa Claus or the Easter Bunny. My father is a pretty big man, but probably not the strongest in the world. And even though I still cherish my mother's kisses, I no longer believe that they have healing power. But, I still believe in Jesus Christ!

We grow out of many things as we grow older. Fairy tales become stories. Parents become human. Healing kisses become love and affection. One thing that remained and will always remain is Who Jesus Christ is. He is the one thing that we will never find out wasn't true!

He is Faithful

To proclaim your love in the morning and your
faithfulness at night. – Psalm 92:2

I read this Psalm and thought how wonderful it would be to do what this verse says everyday. To say every morning, "God, I know this day will be a good day because You love me and will be with me in every step". Then to say every night, "God, thank you for being a part of my day. I was blessed because You were here." This prayer is simple, honest, and true. I heard once that you should say please every morning and thank you every night. I guess in a way, that's what this prayer is.

We might remember to ask God to be with us during the day (some days more than others!). We might remember that His love is never ending and always there. We also need to remember, after His love, strength, and support has gotten us through our day, to say thank you. "To proclaim Your faithfulness at night" – Our God is faithful, so should we be!

꧁ ꧂

January 23

Simply Come

Jesus said, "Come". – Matthew 14:29

When I was little and I would see a commercial for a new toy, I would immediately call out, "Mom, I want that" or in extreme cases, "Mom, I need that!" I still do sometimes, maybe not to my mother, but in my own head. We have an entire advertising industry that has one goal. Their goal is to make us want things we don't need. They go into great detail to tell us that our lives would be so much better is we just had……..

Jesus didn't have an agent. He didn't use gimmicks or catchy slogans. He didn't have to go into great detail or make false promises. He just said, "Come" and people came! For those who responded, they knew that their lives would be so much better just because they had Him!

January 24

Weathering the Storm

You have planted them, yes, they have taken root. – Jeremiah 12:2

I saw a picture with a tree and the words, "The deeper the roots, the higher the reach", below it. I immediately thought of this huge tree that was on the grounds of the church where I grew up. It was supposed to be the biggest tree in the county! Who really knows about that and it doesn't really matter, my point is that this tree was so big that it had to have really deep roots. Over the years, it weathered many storms that pulled most trees right up out of the ground.

We need to have deep roots of faith. In the Parable of the Farmer Scattering Seed, Jesus says, "these have no root, who believe for a while and in time of temptation fall away" (Luke 8:13). In Psalms, it states, "You have brought a vine out of Egypt, planted it, and caused it to take deep root" (Psalm 80:8-9). We can weather the storms of life if our roots are firmly planted in Him. We can reach higher and feel His embrace and peace surround us.

How firmly are you planted in Him? During your next storm, will you make it through safely or will you be pulled up by your roots?

Thank You

Thank you for your love, thank you for your faithfulness.
– Psalm 138:2 (The Message Bible)

One Sunday, our class was discussing gratitude. I immediately thought of a quote I once heard, and will never forget. It goes, "What if all you had tomorrow is what you thanked God for today?" I wish I knew who wrote it, I would love to thank them too! The day I first read that quote, I thanked God for everything I could think of, right down to my shoes! It changed my outlook on thankfulness, and hopefully, I will never forget its lesson. Okay, I've quit thanking Him for my shoes, but I do remember to thank Him for the true blessings in my life, but most of all, I thank Him daily for Him. His love, His salvation, His grace and mercy – I could go on. I thank Him for being the best part of me, the only part that really matters.

We should remember to thank God everyday for all He has done for us. Even in times of strife and struggle, we can always have at least one thing that is good, we have Him! He is all we truly need. Ask yourself today, "What if all you had tomorrow was what you thanked God for today?" Would you be left with much or would you have everything you need?

January 26

The Righteous Will Shine

Then the righteous will shine forth as the sun in the
kingdom of their Father. – Matthew 13:43

When I came into work in the ER one morning, they had just finished cleaning the floors. It had been a week long process of cleaning, waxing, and buffing. As you can imagine, an ER floor gets pretty disgusting with some of the nastiest things you can think of, both seen and unseen, and this cleaning process has to be done periodically. But, when they are finished, you can see the floor shining from anywhere in the room.

In the Old Testament, periodic cleansing had to be done in order to be forgiven of your sins. And when this ritual was over, you were considered clean for a while, but you knew you would have to do it again. Jesus' death on the cross made this periodic cleaning unnecessary. His sacrifice made a way for us to be cleansed in His blood, making our dirty, dingy self "white as snow". When He is finished "the righteous will shine", and others will be able to see it from anywhere in the room!

January 27

Our Loving Heavenly Father

Whoever loves discipline loves knowledge, but he who
hates correction is stupid. – Proverbs 12:1

I was reading Proverbs one night and came across this verse. After laughing about the fact that the Bible uses the word "stupid", I thought about what it means. In my life, there have been periods of time when I was, in fact, stupid. There were times when I would not admit when I was wrong, when I would not admit my mistakes, when I thought I didn't need help or advice from anyone. In these instances, I needed discipline and correction. I needed something to help me not make stupid choices and mistakes.

When I see a parent disciplining their child, I think that must be what it is like when God disciplines us. We will do something that we are not supposed to, or something that could have terrible consequences. When we do, Our Loving Heavenly Father comes and picks us up, slaps our hand, and says "Didn't I warn you not to do that?" God disciplines us because He loves us. He doesn't want us to make mistakes. He doesn't want us to make bad choices. He doesn't want us to be stupid.

The best thing about God's discipline is that when the discipline is over, He folds His arms around us in a big embrace. And He never lets us go!

Sacrifice of Praise

Here am I. Send me! – Isaiah 6:8

Some mornings I wake up 30 minutes before my alarm is set to go off. I wake with a voice saying, "Get up and spend some time with me". I don't always want to. I want those last few minutes of sleep. After ignoring it for a few more minutes I think, "He died for me and I can't get up a little early for Him? I'm pretty pathetic!" So, I get up, grab my Bible, and spent the time reading and praying.

What if Isaiah had said, "Here am I. Send me, but could you not call before noon?" What if Noah had said, "Why don't I wait and see if the rain actually starts before I do all this work?" What if Jesus had said, "You know, that looks like it hurts. I don't like pain so I think I'll just skip it"? Have we become such a selfish society that sacrifice no longer seems possible? Do we claim that we will do anything for our faith, but can't sacrifice anything for Jesus? Do we truly mean it when and if we say, "Here am I. Send me!"

January 29

As Good as It Gets

God will wipe away every tear from their eyes; there will be
no more death, nor sorrow, nor crying. – Revelation 21:4

There are many reasons to feel sorry for those who don't believe. One
reason is because they think that this life is it. This world is as good
as it gets for them. If I thought that, there are times that could be so
depressing that I might have trouble making it through the day!

We, as Christians, can find comfort in the fact that during a bad day,
a bad week, or a bad year; Jesus is with us. We can also find comfort
in the fact that any struggle we face will end – either in this life or
in eternal life with Him. Scripture tells us that "weeping may endure
for a night, but joy comes in the morning" (Psalm 30:5). This is His
promise to us! For us, this life is not as good as it gets!

Always Dependable

If we are not faithful, He will still be faithful, because
He cannot be false to Himself. – 2 Timothy 2:13

I don't like to admit it, but I don't always do what I say I'm going to do. It's often unintentional, I am forgetful sometimes. It's even harder to admit that sometimes it's not. There are some things that I say I will do and after the fact, I just don't want to or find out I can't. I get tired. I can't be in two places at once. And to be honest, sometimes I'm just in the mood to be difficult. What's even worse is that I sometimes do this to Jesus. I tell Him that I will do things or work on this or that, and then I don't end up doing it. Either I don't put enough importance on it and forget, or I realize how difficult it might be and let it fade. I ignore that He and I discussed this matter and move on. Like He forgets!

One of the beautiful and amazing things about Jesus is that no matter what, He is faithful. My disobedience, my difficult mood, my forgetfulness – these don't affect Him. He doesn't work in the "you scratch my back and I'll scratch yours" kind of way. I'm so glad. This doesn't give me an excuse, I know that I need to be more like Him and do what I say I'm going to do. I'm just thankful that even though I'm not always dependable, I have a Savior who is!

Asking for Forgiveness

Therefore I say to you, her sins, which are many, are forgiven, for she loved much. But to whom little is forgiven, the same loves little. - Luke 7:47

In this passage of scripture (Luke 7:36-50), Jesus is dining at the home of a Pharisee. A woman, whom that Pharisee called a sinner, came in weeping, washed Jesus' feet with her tears and dried them with her hair. This is a beautiful story of forgiveness and I encourage you to read it in its entirety. I will try and summarize quickly. The Pharisees did not approve of Jesus letting this "sinner" touch Him. Jesus replied to him, "There was a certain creditor who had two debtors. One owed five hundred denarius, and the other fifty. And when they had nothing with which to repay, he freely forgave them both. Tell Me, therefore, which of them will love him more?"

This woman who knew she needed Jesus humbled herself before Him and asked His forgiveness. He gave it to her. She will never forget His mercy and His grace and she will be changed forever! The Pharisee who didn't think he needed anything......didn't ask!

ᴏᴏ෨ ෨ᴏᴏ

February 1

Loving Him

I am the way, the truth, and the life. – John 14:6

Jesus is the way. If you aren't following Him, then you're following the wrong path. Jesus is the truth. If you hear so-called doctrine that is not of Him, then it's false. Jesus is the life. If your life doesn't include Him, then your life is only an existence.

Jesus said, "You shall love the Lord your God will all your heart, with all your mind" (Matthew 22:37). This means loving Him with completeness. This means loving Him with everything in us. If we learn to love Him like this , He will be our way, our truth, and our life!

Jesus Loves Me

The Lord said, "I have loved you." – Malachi 1:2

When I read this verse, I thought, "Wow!" God's love never ceases to amaze me. Mostly, because He never ceases. He has always loved me. He loved me before my parents did. He loved me before my family and friends did. He loved me before I did anything good or anything bad. He loved me before I even had a name. He loved me so much that 2000 years ago; He died for me on the cross.

Some people think, "Oh, God couldn't possibly love someone like me. I've don't some bad things and made too many mistakes". This is a common misconception. We don't have to earn God's love. We just have to accept it. It's the greatest gift we can ever receive. I say gift because it was purchased by someone else, by Jesus, and was freely given to us. God's love isn't just for good people, it's for all people. It's for those who have faith in Him and trust in Him. Remember the song from childhood, "Jesus Loves Me"? That song is not just for Vacation Bible School, it's for everyday. Accept His gift of love today!

February 3

Spiritual Nourishment

Let the Word of Christ dwell in you richly in all wisdom, teaching and admonishing one another in psalms and hymns and spiritual songs, singing with grace in your hearts to the Lord. - Colossians 3:16

Our pastor once said something that really stuck with me. He was talking about the Word of God and how it is true and powerful and everlasting, this we know. But, he also talked about how the Word of God is "spiritual nourishment". He talked about the fact that our bodies would not be physically healthy if we only ate once a week. If we know that to be true, then why do we think we can be spiritually healthy only getting spiritually nourished once a week? Growing up, I always thought I was doing well because I went to church every week. The problem was, Monday through Saturday, I didn't do much else!

Whether it's studying God's Word, listening to Christian music, praying, or sharing the gospel with a friend, we need spiritual nourishment. It needs to be a part of our daily lives. Some of us are possibly starving for His Word - spiritually anorexic so to speak. The problem is that we probably don't even realize it. Get into His Word. Talk to Him and about Him. Sing His praises. Stop starving yourself and get nourishment at His table!

꧁ ꧂

February 4

Give Me Understanding

Your hands have made me and fashioned me;
give me understanding, that I may learn Your
commandments. - Psalm 119:73

One thing I have learned to do is to ask God for understanding. In the past, if I didn't understand something, I would just ignore it or get angry about it. It's like a small child trying to put a round peg into a square hole. If you watch them, they either get bored and move on to something else, or they have a fit and throw that round peg across the room.

God wants us to understand His ways. He wants us to know His will for our lives. How do we get this understanding, by asking Him to give it to us? Two other verses came to mind when I was reading this psalm; "If any of you lacks wisdom, let him ask of God, who gives to all liberally and without reproach, and it will be given to him" (James 1:5), and "Lord, I believe; help my unbelief" (Mark 9:24). If you don't understand, ask Him about it. If your belief is wavering, ask for His help. Don't give up or throw your peg across the room, pray for God to "give me understanding"!

He Wipes Our Tears

God will wipe away every tear from their eyes; there shall be
no more death, nor sorrow, nor crying. – Revelation 21:4

Do you ever think that no one understands the pain you are going through or that the stress in your life is more than anyone should have to bear? Do you ever feel alone, misunderstood, or sad? At one time or another, everyone has felt this way.

As a child of God, you are never alone in your pain, stress, or sadness. God is always ready to listen and to give a comforting embrace. He is always there, period! He wipes our tears, calms our stress, and can turn our sadness into joy! Do you feel alone today? Are you hurting beyond what you think you can bear? Do you have tears that won't stop flowing? Call on Him today!

ༀ ༀ ༀ

February 6

Undivided Attention

I will sing praises with the whole of my being. – Psalm 108:1

Have you ever had a conversation with someone and you didn't feel like they were really listening? Isn't it frustrating that you don't have their undivided attention, especially if what you are saying is important to you. Think about how God feels when we are in church, in His house. How many of us spend part of the service thinking about where to have lunch, how much work we have to do on Monday, about how the song isn't the type like? How many of us concentrate on the fact that the sermon went five minutes too long?

This Psalm says it all, "I will sing praises with the whole of my being." We are to worship God with everything we have. I'm positive He deserves it. Give Him your undivided attention in worship and let all else go for just a little while. I'm sure you will leave a whole lot better than when you went in!

ᴄ๑ໄ๑ ໄ๑ᴄ

February 7

He Doesn't Know Them

Lord, you bless those who do what is right. - Psalm 5:12

Have any of you ever been taught a lesson by God? I have. I will mess up and mess up, and He has to come in and straighten everything out. But, when I seem to get it right, He sees that I am blessed. The Beatitudes in Matthew 5 are all about how we are blessed if we do this or do that. If we show mercy, we get mercy.....If we give forgiveness, forgiveness is given.....If we stand up for God, He will stand up for us. If we follow His commandments and show love, we are blessed and filled with His peace and joy. If we don't, we are not. It's simple really. If we are outside of God's will, He will do what He can to bring us back!

I have thought from time to time that certain people seem to be so blessed and they don't even know God? They mess up and don't seem to reap the consequences. They do whatever they want and however they want and nothing happens. The sad truth is, they don't get lessons from God. Why? It's because He doesn't know them! They will get their one and final lesson from God when He says, "I never knew you, depart from Me!" (Matthew 7:23). I don't know about you, but I'm glad I'm getting my lessons along the way and will be eternally blessed!

February 8

He is the Way

I will bring the blind by a way they did not know; I will lead
them in paths they have not known. I will make darkness
light before them, and crooked places straight. These things
I will do for them, and not forsake them. - Isaiah 42:16

I can remember going through a couple of haunted houses when I
was a teenager. It was so dark, I couldn't see where I was going. There
were strange voices and scary images popping up all around me. I
kept bumping into things while searching for a way out. Ultimately,
when I was about to completely freak out, I could see that the end
was coming - why? Because I could see the light!

Jesus can bring us out of our dark places. He can shine a light around
us and help us find our way. No more bumping into obstacles or
searching down the wrong road. Don't freak out - call on Him. He
is the right path! He is the light! He is the way!

Hearing What You Hear

He who has ears to hear, let him hear! - Matthew 11:15

There are many phrases used when someone is trying to get your attention. "Listen up!", "Hey, I'm talking to you", or "Please be quite!" Jesus said, "He who has ears to hear, let him hear!" This is said at least 8 times in the Gospels, and that many times again in Revelation. This is Jesus saying, "Hey, pay attention to this, it's important!"

Sometimes, we hear without hearing. Something, as they say it, "goes in one ear and out the other". We not only need to hear, but listen in order to understand. We need to read or hear the Word of God, not just as an interesting topic, but as an application. We need to hear, listen, and do. Our hearing needs action. When you hear Jesus say, "He who has ears to hear, let him hear" - pay attention, it's important, and He's talking to you!

Spiritual Eyes

"Blessed are the eyes which see the things you see." - Luke 10:23

I was recently reading an article* about Jennifer Hudson. She's a Grammy winning artist, an Oscar winning actress, and well on her way to "fame and fortune". But all the fame and all the money in the world couldn't stop the tragedy that awaited her when her mother, her brother, and her nephew were murdered. In this article, she speaks of her faith and how God sustained her. She even has a new song entitled, "You Pulled Me Through". One thing she said that was quoted in this article struck me. She said, "Too often we look at things through human eyes. But when you look at the world spiritually, it makes far more sense. I don't think I would be here without it". I don't know this woman and I don't know about her faith, but thought her words rang true.

I often try to humanize my faith, and put human limitations on God. When I take away my tendency to mess up, to over think, or just plain get it wrong, and look through "spiritual eyes", I get it. I see through the eyes of the light and love of Jesus.

It's impossible to stay angry, to keep wondering why, or to let bitterness set in if you are seeing through the eyes of Jesus. Seeing through His eyes will allow you to understand what "blessed are the eyes which see what you see" truly means!

* The article referenced in this devotional came from "Entertainment Weekly", #1042, April 10, 2009

February 11

What is Mercy?

Blessed are the merciful, for they will be shown mercy. - Matthew 5:7

I'm often amazed at how much I don't know. I study and I think that I'm doing pretty well, then I get asked an easy question that I should know and I can't answer. When I was teaching youth, one of the girls asked me what mercy was. They are preparing for a mission trip and were told that they needed to be able to define words such as "grace," "salvation," and "mercy." I got stuck on mercy. What is it? Being nice when you don't have to? Not giving a punishment that is due? Loving the unlovable? I, obviously, stumbled through that night, but decided that I, along with my girls, would get prepared.

The definition of mercy is, "kind and gentle treatment of someone having no right to it". Okay, that I get. Jesus said, "Blessed are the merciful, for they will be shown mercy". I'm taking that to mean if I show mercy (kind and gentle treatment of someone having no right to it), then He will do the same for me! Now that we know what mercy is and that is easily explained, but you know what else? It is also easily shown!

Who Needs Jesus?

I have not come to call the righteous, but
sinners, to repentance. - Luke 5:32

I overheard a conversation while standing in line. Two women were obviously talking negatively about someone. In the end of the conversation, one of the women said, "Well, they just need them some Jesus!" Well, I agree with what she said, but also thought, doesn't she? Don't I? Doesn't everybody?

Paul tells us in Romans, "The righteousness from God comes through faith in Jesus Christ to all who believe. There is no difference, for all have sinned and fall short of the glory of God, and are justified freely by his grace through the redemption that came by Christ Jesus" (Romans 3:22-24). So, since we are all sinners, we all need Jesus. When Jesus said, "I have not come to call the righteous, but sinners, to repentance", He meant everyone! In other words, we all "need us some Jesus!"

ೂ⊙ ☙ಌ

February 13

Anytime, Anywhere

Pray without ceasing. - 1 Thessalonians 5:17

I once had a discussion with someone about prayer. Questions came up as to what we should pray for and what we shouldn't. I told them to pray about everything, that the Bible tells us to. "Be anxious for nothing, but IN EVERYTHING by prayer and supplication...." (Philippians 4:6-emphasis added). I went on to say that prayer, to me, is like a conversation with my dearest friend. I talk about important things with my best friend. I talk about concerns, fears, and annoyances with my best friend. But I also talk about silly, uncomplicated things with my best friend. I'm just sharing myself with Him, with my dear friend.

Just like there is not "in case of emergency" seal on the Bible, there is no check list to seek before prayer. It's for anytime, anywhere. If it's important to you, it's important to Jesus. If it concerns you, He wants you to talk to Him about it. If it's just something you want to share, He's overjoyed that you want to share it with Him. He is ready to listen, no matter what it is!

February 14

Perfect Love

Love keeps no record of wrongs. – 1 Corinthians 13:5

Have you ever done something that those around you won't ever let you forget? Have you made a mistake that you will forever be remembered for? Do you have regrets that others, even yourself, won't let you move on from?

The perfect love of Jesus is an amazing blessing. Once you have asked for His forgiveness, it's done and forgotten. This sin, this mistake, this regret no longer exists. This world may often remind you of what you have done, but Jesus doesn't. This world my replay your mistakes over and over again, but Jesus doesn't. This world might keep a "record of your wrongs", but Jesus doesn't. His love is unconditional and it wipes the slate clean!

February 15

Sacrifice What?

No one takes (My life) from me, but I lay it down of Myself. – John 10:18

I was talking to my class of high school girls and the topic was on sacrifice. We are Baptist and therefore don't, as a denomination, observe Lent, but it was the time of year that got us on the topic. We were all talking about things we might give up for 40 days. They were all listing things that I'm pretty sure weren't that important to them. I looked at them and said, "What about giving up Facebook for 40 days? Or Texting?" For some of them, you would have thought I had asked them to cut off their arms! Smiling back, I said, "Now that is what sacrifice is!"

Sacrifice is something we all struggle with because it's a choice. We usually don't chose to give up something that means a lot to us. It might be a relationship that isn't encouraging your walk with Christ. It might be a job that sometimes makes us compromise our beliefs. It might be a habit we can't quite kick and you've quit trying. Whatever it is, it isn't easy, that's why it's called sacrifice! Jesus gave Himself for us, what will we give Him today?

Stop, Drop, and Pray

"Lord, teach us to pray." - Luke 11:1

I'm amazed at the times I fail to stop and pray. One day, I was worried about something, playing the "what if" game and at that moment, my cell phone beeped letting me know I had a text message. The text was a verse, "I can do all things through Christ who gives me strength" (Philipians 4:13) and that's all it said. That's all I needed. I know that verse by heart, but it took a reminder in the form of a text message for me to stop and pray. When I don't pray in times of stress, it would be like running around if I was on fire, when all I would need to do is just stop, drop, and roll.

Jesus teaches me in many ways and is always there for me. All I have to do is reach out my hand. He even uses modern technology to say, "Hey, I'm here. Talk to Me. I promise I can make this easier!" I guess what I'm trying to say is; don't run around fretting and not knowing what to do. The next time you're on fire, don't' run around in circles, making it worse; just stop, drop, and pray!

ᲐᏋ ᎨᎯ

February 17

He is With Me

I am with you always. – Matthew 28:20

When I was little and got scared in the middle of the night, I would go get my mother and she would come get in bed with me. I can remember reaching out in the darkness and putting my hand on her back. The fact that I could feel her presence helped me fall right back to sleep. The monsters could not get me and the nightmares didn't return if my mom was there!

As I have grown, I have realized that monsters don't always come in ugly, hairy forms and that nightmares can happen when I am awake. Monsters and nightmares can be real and can come after me!

I can take comfort that Jesus is always with me. If I run to Him when I'm scared, He is bigger than my fears (Psalm 23:4). If I go to Him when I'm tired, He will give me rest (Matthew 11:28). If I have worked myself up about something, He can come and give me peace (John 14:27). I don't have to reach out my hand in the darkness, I know He is there!

ৡৡ ৢৢ

February 18

Gift of Love

Then Mary took a pound of very costly spikenard, an
expensive perfume; and poured it on Jesus' feet and
wiped His feet with her hair. And the house was filled
with the fragrance of the perfume. – John 12:3

After hearing a sermon on this passage, I thought about what gifts
I give to Jesus. In this story in John, Mary gave an extravagant gift
to Jesus. She not only poured out this very valuable perfume on His
feet, and then wiped them dry with her hair. She was giving a gift
of love to Him

Many times I get focused on what Jesus is doing for me that I rarely
take time to look at my side of the relationship. It makes me think
about the fact that when I really care about someone, the gifts I give
them are thought out, from the heart, and usually cost more than
one I just pick up in a hurry. When someone means something to
me, I try to give them a gift that I think will make them happy. I
try to pick out something that reminds me of them. These gifts don't
always cost a lot financially, but they do take time and effort on my
part. No matter the gift, it's a gesture of love from me to them.

Mary gave a gift of love to Jesus when she anointed His feet with
extravagant oil. I guess what I'm asking myself today is, "What gift
of love am I giving Him today?" What about you?

❀❀❀

February 19

I'm Ready

Let the peace of God rule in your hearts. - Colossians 3:15

When do you have peace? Is it when everything is going your way? Probably not. When everything is going my way, I can sometimes still wait for everything to disappear, be taken, or just change. I can't even enjoy what I have because I fear what will happen next. Sustaining peace comes not from our circumstances, but from having God's peace in our hearts. When we let Him have control over our lives and we trust in His will and His way, peace comes in and stays.

Getting out of God's way has been major problem in my life. I give over, and then I take back. I say I trust, and then still try to do things my own way. I fervently pray, "Not my will, but yours", but then end it with, "but if you're open to suggestions, I have some great ideas of what Your will should be!" I sometimes seem to be in a constant state of tug of war with my human selfishness and my spiritual willingness. Peace finally comes when I say, "Okay God, mold me in Your will and way, I'm ready!"

⊙℗℗℗℗℗

February 20

Strength in Weakness

*When my spirit grows faint within me, it is you
who know my way. - Psalm 142:3*

I'm not always strong, but I'm not always weak either. Being human, I tend to waver. I don't always make the right choices for my life or know the best way to go. But, there are times when I do get it right. The sad part is I can't always tell which time is which. I can make a choice today, only to find out tomorrow that it was wrong. That's where Jesus helps. I have to trust that if I'm praying, the decisions I'm making are the right ones. If I'm walking His path, I won't get lost on my journey. If I do mess up, He can pick me up and set me straight.

We will get tired and weak. We will get lost a few times in this journey called life. It's such a blessing that we have the One that is strength in our weakness, is wisdom in our ignorance, and is light that helps us find our way!

෨ල ௦෨

February 21

Yes, You Can

"But Lord," Gideon asked, "how can I save Israel? My clan is the weakest in Manasseh, and I am the least in my family." - Judges 6:15

Gideon wasn't a warrior or a prince. He wasn't a bright and shining star. He was so unsure of himself that he questioned God's choice a few times, asking for a sign to make sure he wasn't about to run into certain death. He didn't feel competent to fulfill the task that God was asking him to do. But, God said, "I will be with you" (Judges 6:16). In other words, God was saying, "Yes, you can!" And with God by his side, Gideon defeated the Midianites (who were oppressing his people) and became a judge of Israel.

We may not always feel equipped to do what God wants us to do. We wouldn't be, without Him. If we are willing to trust, if we have faith in His word, and if we have the obedience to step out, even in uncertainty; it's amazing what we can do. The next time you are thinking, "Lord, I can't", listen and hear Him say, "Yes, you can!"

Take His Hand

"Sir," the invalid replied, "I have no one to help me into the pool when the water is stirred. While I am trying to get in, someone else goes down ahead of me." - John 5:7

In this passage of scripture, it talks of a pool that was believe to have healing waters. The blind, lame, and paralyzed would come to lie in it. People of that time believed that an angel came down to stir the waters and the sick would be healed. As this man, an invalid of 38 years, tried to get to these waters, he had no idea who had come to stand beside him. He was scrambling to get to this pool, when, standing right beside him was the Great Physician was an arms length away. Jesus asked him, "Do you want to get well?"(John 5:6). Then after hearing this man's reply (above 5:7), Jesus said, "Get up! Pick up your mat and walk" (John 5:8).

Sometimes we try things the hard way. We will drag ourselves through myths and so-called remedies in order to seek healing, love, grace and peace; when the true way, the true light, is standing right beside us. Jesus is right here with us - reach out and take His hand!

February 23

Listing Qualities

Life in not defined by what you have, even when you
have a lot. - Luke 12:15 (The Message Bible)

I'm single, so people are always thinking of someone special for me.
I get it everywhere I go. Family reunions are not always my favorite
time. It's like people feel the need to remind me that I'm not married.
Although, this isn't always family, it can even be a stranger I meet
in passing. "I'm going to find somebody for you", is a common
promise in my life. Although, I appreciate them thinking of me, I
get amused sometimes at the descriptions I get. A list of qualities is
given to me just like they are checking off a list. Through years of
this, I have learned that if the first things they list about a person is
what they do for a living or how much money they have, then there's
usually not much else to talk about. It's like the old joke, if you hear,
"They've got a great personally", it usually means "be careful, and
don't look"!

The substance of a person is not in what they drive or in what they
do, but in Who drives them, and for Whom they do what they
do. While success is never, in itself, a bad characteristic, it might
need to be listed as an afterthought not a driving force. While
my preferences have definitely changed over the years, now, if I
don't hear, "He's a Christian" first, I tend to stop listening. I guess
my question this morning is, if someone were describing you, what
would be listed first?

February 24

Believing

Jesus said, "You believe because I told you I saw you under the
fig tree. You shall see greater things than that." - John 1:50

When Jesus was calling His disciples, Philip brought Nathanael
to Him. Jesus knew Nathanael already. When asked how, Jesus
said, "I could see you under the fig tree before Philip found you".
Nathanael replied, "Rabbi, you are the Son of God; You are the
King of Israel" (John 1:48-49). He believed in a moment. That's all
it took!

After reading this passage in John, it reminded me of the passage about
the rich man and Lazarus (Luke 16:19-31). Both the rich man and
Lazarus died. The rich man went to hell and Lazarus went to heaven.
The rich man begged Abraham that Lazarus be allowed to show
himself raised from the dead to the rich man's family, so they would
believe and not end up in the same torment the rich man found
himself in now. And Abraham replied, "If they do not listen to
Moses and the Prophets, they will not be convinced even if someone
rises from the dead".

These two stories tell the same truth. Jesus is the way, the truth and
the life (John 14:6). You will either believe that, or you won't!

ᴄ᷒ᴏ ᴏ᷒ᴄ

February 25

Higher Thoughts

As the heavens are higher than the earth, so are My ways higher than your ways and My thoughts than your thoughts. - Isaiah 55:9

I don't know about any of you, but I usually think my thoughts and ideas are pretty good. I don't think of myself as a stupid person or a reckless person. I don't sit down and think, "I wonder how much I can screw up my life today?" or "I think this is the worst possible choice for me, so that's what I'll pick." I have made some pretty bad choices over the years and I have never intended the outcomes I experienced. That is one of the many reasons I need Jesus!

We make choices everyday. Jesus needs to be a part of your decision making process. We might not always understand His ways. We won't always like what is happening in our lives. We might not always be on the same page as Him. But, we do have to remember that "As the heavens are higher than the earth, so are My ways higher than your ways and My thoughts than your thoughts", says the Lord!

ॐ

February 26

He'll Fix It

He bore the sin of many, and made intercession
for the transgression. - Isaiah 53:12

One day, I was having lunch with a friend. We ordered, paid, and were waiting for our food. Soon, my order was up and ready and my friend's was not. We waited a few more minutes, and then finally asked if it had been forgotten, and it had. There had been a mix up somewhere in the food preparation process. The woman behind the counter kept saying, "Well, I don't know what happened, but it wasn't my fault." Blame really wasn't an issue. I think it would have gone much better if she had said, "I'm so sorry about that, let me fix it."

With Jesus, blame wasn't an issue. He didn't look at my sin and say, "Well, I didn't do it!" He didn't point a finger with a "Don't look at me, this is your fault" stare. Instead, He spread out His arms on a cross and said, "Let Me fix it!"

February 27

Faithful and Righteous

Faithfulness springs forth from the earth, and righteousness
looks down from heaven. - Psalm 85:11

When I read the above verse, I loved the story it tells, the picture it draws in my head. I pictured my hands reaching up toward Heaven, having faith that He will take my hands. That my faithful act of believing in Him, makes His righteousness rain down on me. It made me think of the words of Paul, "the righteousness which is from God by faith" (Philippians 3:9).

Remember that He is always faithful and righteous. Remember, that "every good and perfect gift is from above" (James 1:17). So therefore, let your faithfulness spring forth from the earth, as His righteousness comes down!

February 28

Hand it Over

Give all your worries to Him, because He
cares about you. - 1 Peter 5:7

I have a dear friend that sings with me at church. Sometimes, when she sings a solo, she gets fiercely nervous. She has a certain ritual that she usually does with her mother before she sings, but one time her mother wasn't there, so I had to fill in. Before she stepped out of the choir, she "gave me her nerves". Which is basically, handing me something imaginary and I pretend to take it. I held on to her nerves until she was finished and came back to sit down. This helps her, so I was glad to help. Actually, I'm thinking about using this technique myself!

This is exactly what we should be doing with Jesus, not in the form of an imaginary game, but for real. We should hand all of our worries, fears, and concerns over to Him. He will not only hold on to them for us, but He truly does make everything better. He gives peace and calm when we need it. So, whatever it is in your life - hand it over!

Something Stronger

I know your deeds. See, I have placed before you an open door that no one can shut. I know that you have little strength, yet you have kept my word and have not denied my name. - Revelation 3:8

The above verse was a part of the letter that John was asked to write to the church of Philadelphia in the Revelation of Jesus. This church was suffering through persecution. They were not conforming to the ways of the world in a time when it was dangerous not to do so. But, they had "little strength." In reading that part of this verse, I was reminded of "My grace is sufficient for you, for My power is made perfect in weakness" (2 Corinthians 12:9). Jesus said to them, "Since you have kept my command to endure patiently, I will also protect you." John MacArthur (Bible commentary writer) said this about the church of Philadelphia, "This is a faithful, Christ- honoring, and zealous, missionary-minded church that is alive with the flame of evangelism and in love with Jesus Christ. This is the kind of church that brings glory to God."

Being weak is not always a bad thing. Being weak makes us have to depend on something stronger. This church while being weak was also described as "in love with Jesus Christ and the kind of church that brought glory to God." Why? Because in their weakness, they drew strength from something much stronger - they drew strength from Jesus. Where do you draw your strength from?

March 2

Walking in Fire

"Look!" he answered, "I see four men loose, walking in
the midst of the fire; and they are not hurt, and the form
of the fourth is like the Son of God." - Daniel 3:25

I was reading this passage in Daniel yesterday. I love the story of
Shadrach, Meshach, and Aded-Nego. They refused to worship any
god (or king) but the God of Israel. For this, king Nebuchadnezzar
had them cast into a fiery furnace. And just to make sure, he asked
that the furnace be heated seven times more than usual. The fire was
so hot, that those who were commanded to throw these men into the
fire were killed because of the fierce heat. But, Shadrach, Meshach,
and Abed-Nego didn't even get singed. Not their clothes.....Not their
hair.....Not their skin.....Nothing. Then, comes my favorite part of
this story, the king, after looking into the furnace, rose and asked,
"Did we not cast three men bound into the midst of the fire?" Those
around him answered, "True, O King." Then the king replied,
"Look!" he answered, "I see four men loose, walking in the midst of
the fire; and they are not hurt, and the form of the fourth is like the
Son of God" (Daniel 3:24-25).

What did I take from this story? If Jesus is in my heart, it doesn't
matter how many binds this world puts around me, He can break
them. And no matter what fiery furnace I'm thrown into, He is right
there with me, walking in the midst of the fire!

March 3

The Devil is in the Details

*The One who is in you is greater than the one
who is in the world. - 1 John 4:4*

I was watching a TV show and the old saying, "The devil is in the details" was quoted. I had never really given that phrase much thought before. Isn't it just a quip like many others we have used over the years? Maybe not.

The devil IS in the details. He knows what he's doing. He doesn't jump up and down screaming, "Here I come to tempt you! Are you ready?" No, he slithers in like a snake, unnoticed and unannounced until he strikes. It's the small details of life, which we don't often pay attention to, that he can use against us. Things like, "one drink won't hurt anything", "I was just flipping channels and it was there, so I'll just stop and watch for a second", or "I know he's married, but flirting won't hurt anything." Like I said, the devil is in the details!

Scripture tells us, "I will rescue you from your own" (Acts 26:17). We may be no match for Satan and his tactics, but Jesus is. That is why we need to bring things both big and small to Him. The details of our lives matter. Jesus is our only line of defense!

Joy in Trials

My brethren, count it all joy when you fall into various trials, knowing
that the testing of your faith produces patience. – James 1:2-3

Once in Sunday School, we were talking about faith in the hard
times. I thought of these verses. The first time I read them I thought,
"Yeah, right!" Then in realizing what my "hard times" have done
for and in me, I could see exactly what he meant. It's through some
of the hardest situations I've been through that my faith was able
to grow and become something I can depend on. Something I now
consider a blessing. It's because I've gone through trials that I am
the person I am today. This is true for everyone. You will change in
trials, the question is – will it be for the better or worse? The outcome
of this question depends on your faith!

If faith is never tested, then how do you know its strength? If life is
always rosy, what's the point? In writing this, two passages in Isaiah
come to mind, "But those who wait upon the Lord shall renew their
strength; they shall mount up with wings of eagles, they shall run
and not be weary, the shall walk and not faint" (Isaiah 40:31) and
"Fear not, for I have redeemed you; I have called you by your name;
you are Mine. When you pass through the waters, I will be with you.
When you walk through the fire, you shall not be burned, nor shall
the flame scorch you. You are precious in My sight" (Isaiah 43:1-4).
In your tough times, don't shun Jesus and dwell on the "why me?"
that all of us ask. Instead, draw close to Him and He will draw close
to you!

ᕫᕤᕫᕤᕫᕤ

March 5

He Can Make You Beautiful

He has made everything beautiful in its time. – Ecclesiastes 3:11

If you are like me, your life has not always been beautiful. Not in the terms of this world, and certainly not in the beautifying image of Christ. One of the numerous wonderful things about Jesus is that He can transform you into a thing of beauty. He can take an ugly piece of pottery that has been shattered to pieces and make it a glorious vessel. All you have to do is let Him.

It was at the point of giving my life to Christ, not just accepting His salvation, but truly saying, "Here you go. I've made a mess of things, but the rubble that is left is Yours;" that He transformed me into something that He sees as beautiful. I still tend to get in His way sometimes, but my intention is always to let Him mold me. I don't have to be perfect for Christ, but I do try to be willing and available to Him. I need to always remember that He gave me beauty for ashes, gladness instead of mourning, and a garment of praise instead of a spirit of despair (Isaiah 61:3). When I let Him, His beauty can shine through me!

March 6

Be of Good Cheer

In the world you will have tribulation; but be of good
cheer, I have overcome the world. – John 16:33

Have you ever had a problem and when someone tried to help, you said, "You have no idea what I'm going through?" I can remember getting angry with those who would say, "I know how hard this is," when I knew they had no idea. It's so hard to go through something when you feel alone, excluded, and without someone who can relate.

Jesus can help us in any situation. He has been tempted with all this world has to offer. He has been beaten and bruised. He has been misunderstood and mocked. He has an idea of what you are going through. He can imagine how hard it is for you. He is always with you. He can look at you, show His nail scarred hands, and say, "Be of good cheer, I have overcome the world!"

Because of Love

Your life is now hidden with Christ in God. - Colossians 3:3

I know all of you have seen a child hide behind their parents. I did it when I was a child. You did too. There was a sense of safety behind your parent, holding on to their legs. No one could get around that shield of protection! Most of the time, the child will take a peak with a look like; "Let me see you get through this!" Somehow, most children instinctively know that their parents would do anything to protect them, to keep them from getting hurt, or to shield them from pain. Why? Because of love.

This is what I thought of when I read the above verse. When we accept Christ as our Savior, we become a part of His family. We die to the world and become alive in Him. He becomes Our Heavenly Father. And somehow, we instinctively know that He would do anything to protect us, to keep us from getting hurt, or to shield us from pain. Why? Because of love!

Everlasting to Everlasting

From everlasting to everlasting.... - Psalm 103:17

We are all constrained by time. Our daily schedules are made up of pieces of time that are planned out for this or for that. Our physical lives are made up of years. Our relationships are counted by weeks, then months, then years. Everything in this world is centered around time. "What time is it?" might be the most commonly asked question we hear. I think that we are so bound by time that it is hard for us to grasp that time isn't an issue for God. "From everlasting to everlasting," He has been around and He has known us and He has loved us.

Scripture tells us "do not forget this one thing, that with the Lord, one day is as a thousand years, and a thousand years as one day" (2 Peter 3:8). When you think of "everlasting to everlasting," today's problems might seem a little less severe, tomorrow's worries might seem a little less scary, and yesterday's mistakes might seem a little dimmer!

March 9

God's Gifts

For by grace you have been saved through faith, and
that not of yourselves; it is a gift of God, not of works,
lest anyone should boast. – Ephesians 2:8-9

Have you ever received an invitation to a party and at the bottom is printed, "No Gifts Please"? I'm always going to bring one anyway. Why? It's not because that person necessarily deserves a gift, did something remarkable, or even earned one. I do it because I want to. Because I want to show that person that I care about them. Because I love to give gifts. These gifts are always accepted with a smile and a "Thank you, but it wasn't necessary." I always follow with, "Well, yes it was and I wanted to".

So many people focus on the fact that they don't deserve God's love, His salvation, or His blessings. If we all waited to deserve it, it would never happen to any of us. That is why blessings are sometimes called gifts. Gifts are not something we deserve. Gifts are not something we earn. Gifts are not something that we have to bear the cost of. Gifts are given from someone else to us, usually because they care about us.

Don't place on God's invitation into your life a "No Gifts Please" clause, because you don't think you deserve them. Just except them with a smile and a "Thank you, but it wasn't necessary." Jesus will answer with, "Well, yes it was and I wanted to".

March 10

Heart of Forgiveness

*"Father, forgive them, for they do not know
what they are doing." – Luke 23:34*

Forgiveness. It's a hard pill to swallow sometimes. I think it's the most freeing thing we have, but the most difficult to do. We don't want to forgive those who have hurt us. We don't want to give them another chance. We don't want to let go of the anger because it might make us weak.

Jesus, as He was dying on the cross, asked His Father to forgive those who were killing Him. This is amazing to me. We find it hard to forgive someone for talking behind our backs or making fun of us in front of our friends. We can't seem to forgive someone for doing something that they might not have even known they did. Jesus was mocked, falsely accused, and killed. It was intentional, but He still had a heart of forgiveness!

Daily Prayers

Give us this day, our daily bread. - Matthew 6:11

Why is daily prayer needed? I don't know about you, but sometimes my needs, wants, fears, circumstances, and problems occur and change on a daily basis. Maybe not some things, but this world never stops moving, and I haven't stopped being a part of it yet, so my prayers don't need to stop being lifted up.

Praying "give us this day, our daily bread" is asking that He give you what you need when you need it, having faith that He will be there to give it, and believing that His love and His will never fails!

March 12

What Matters?

*The earth and everything in it, the world and its
inhabitants, belong to the Lord. - Psalm 24:1*

There is a long running joke in Baptist churches, possibly every
church, about people claiming seats. It's actually not much of a
joke because I have heard many stories of how visitors would not
return to a church because a member was mean to them for sitting
in their seat. How ridiculous is that? We have no ownership of seats
or anything else in a church. What we do have ownership of is our
actions. In how we treat others. In what part of Jesus shines through
us.

This world and everything in it belongs to the Lord. Every person in
this world is special to Him. What do you think will matter more
to Jesus, if you sit in the same seat every Sunday in church or if you
often have someone who didn't know Him in the seat beside you?

ૐૐ ૐૐ

March 13

Clothe Yourselves

Therefore, as God's chosen people, holy and dearly
loved, clothe yourselves with compassion, kindness,
humility, gentleness and patience. - Colossians 3:12

Have you ever looked up the definitions of these characteristics that
Paul says we are to have? This is what Webster's had to say about it.
Compassion - a deep awareness of and sympathy of another's suffering.
Kindness - the quality of being warmhearted, considerate, humane
and sympathetic. Humility -a lack of false pride. Gentleness - also
sometimes called "meekness," mildness of manners or disposition.
And last, Patience - also sometimes called "longsuffering," good-
natured tolerance of delay or incompetence. Wow!

When you break each of these characteristics down, you see that
they aren't just some words picked out at random. These are
characteristics of Jesus. This verse tells us to "clothe yourselves"
with these characteristics. Clothes are a covering for our bodies.
Ephesians tells us to, "put on the full armor of God, so you may be
able to stand your ground" (6:13). It's not human nature to always
show compassion, kindness, humility, gentleness, and patience, but
it is His nature. When clothed in His love and salvation, these can
become your nature too!

March 14

Running the Race

Let us run with endurance the race that is set before us, looking
unto Jesus, the author and finisher of our faith. - Hebrews 12:1

A friend of mine is competing in a race this weekend. A part of this
race is swimming, part biking, and part running. It will take a long
time. We were thinking of all the things she will need to take with
her during this race that will take hours to finish. We were thinking
of bug spray, sun screen, water, food, chapstick, and this list went
on and on. Finally, she said, I can only carry the essentials with me.
There isn't room for anything else.

Just as an athlete will strip away anything unnecessary before
competing in a race, as Christians, so should we. We need to rid
ourselves of anything that will ensnare us, slow us down, or get in
our way. This verse talks about endurance, a steady determination to
keep going, no matter how much you might want to stop or give up.
Jesus will be strength in our weakness, patience in our frustration,
and our biggest supporter along the way. He is our essential. This
world gives you plenty of reasons to quit living for Christ, but stand
firm in your faith and finish the race!

March 15

One Act

If by the one man's offense many died, much more the
grace of God and the gift by the grace of the one Man,
Jesus Christ, abounded to many. – Romans 5:15

Have you ever had one event change your life forever? It could be
a good event or a bad one. Maybe you are thinking of the day you
received Christ as your Savior. Maybe you are thinking about the
day you got married, had a child, or graduated from college. These
types of things change who you are forever, hopefully in a good
way. You could also be thinking about the day you made a horrible
mistake, either accidental or the consequence of a bad choice. These
can also change who you are forever, depending on the aftermath.
One thing – One instance – One moment – can change the course
of, not just your life, but sometimes can affect the lives of those
around you.

I have no doubt in my mind that Adam and Eve had no idea of the
repercussions of their actions when they ate the forbidden fruit. I
believe in my heart that they had no intention of damning themselves
and future generations to a life of hardships and unavoidable death.
But, that is exactly what their choice brought to the world. On the
other hand, there is Christ. His actions were not accidental. He was
not confused about what He was doing. He knew the outcome of
what His actions would bring. They brought hope! He gave back
to us the life that was taken away by the first sin. He gave Himself
for us. His one act, His unselfish sacrifice, His unconditional love
– saved the world!

ﻬﻬ ﻬﻬ

March 16

His Suffering

He was pierced for our rebellion, crushed for our sin. – Isaiah 53:5

This scripture by Isaiah was written about 681 BC. There are many detailed prophesies about the crucifixion. About Jesus' life, birth to death. The people of Israel knew the Savior was coming. They also knew why He was coming, because of them (us). Because of their (our) sin. Someone had to pay the price for our rebellion, for our sins. Jesus paid that price. He was "pierced" for our rebellion, "crushed" for our sins.

My sins are forgiven because of Him. Because of the sacrifice of His life. Because of the suffering He endured on the cross. Because of the fulfillment of His death and resurrection. Because of His love, I have life!

March 17

Doubting Thomas

Then He said to Thomas, "Put your finger here; see
my hands. Reach out your hand and put it into my
side. Stop doubting and believe." – John 20:27

Surely, we have all heard the phrase, "doubting Thomas". I think
that sometimes we are a little hard on Thomas. He was only doing
what Christians have done through the ages, he doubted. Although,
we may not doubt that Jesus is who He said He is, but we have all
doubted what He can do.

When you feel that Jesus is leading you to do something, have you
ever said, "That's impossible", "You're asking too much", or "I'm not
equipped to do that"? When we say these things, we, in fact, doubt
Jesus. We are saying that there are things He cannot do. "I can do
all things through Christ who strengthens me" (Philippians 4:13).
When are we going to stop doubting and believe in Him?

March 18

The Winning Team

If God is for us, who can be against us? – Romans 8:31

If any of you are like me, you are very competitive. I always like to be on the winning team. It's just no fun to lose. As a Christian, we don't have to listen to forecasted predictions, we win! The Bible tells us so. Jesus said, "In this world, you will have trouble. But take heart! I have overcome the world" (John 16:33). Our Team Captain, Jesus, has defeated our enemy at the grave, and will beat him again in the end.

Though sometimes I feel like Satan is way ahead, I know we come back with a vengeance and this battle won't go into over time. It will just be over! Then, we will be doing our victory dance in Heaven!

March 19

Dying to Self

I tell you the truth, unless a kernel of wheat falls to the
ground and dies, it remains only a single seed. But if
it dies, it produces many seeds. – John 12:24

In this verse, Jesus is talking about how His death will save others.
He could have been selfish and said, "I'm not going through with
this!" He could have still been a great man in history, but only that.
He didn't choose that path. He sacrificed Himself, His life, for us.
He had to die so we could live.

Unless it's some extreme circumstance, we don't have to physically
die for our faith. We do, however, have to die to self. We have to
think bigger than ourselves. It would be easier some nights, to go
home and rest instead of going to choir practice or Bible study. It
would be less hectic some mornings, to just go back to bed instead
of getting up and going to church. It would be less awkward to just
talk about today's current events, than to share the gospel with a lost
friend. We sometimes have to sacrifice comfort and convenience for
our faith. Dying to self will produce many seeds!

ᷧ᷉ᷧ

March 20

What's Best

In humility, consider others as more important
than yourselves. – Philippians 2:3

We live in a society that is "me" driven. What we want....What we need....What we think....How many books are written, T-shirts worn, and magnets bought that advertise, "It's all about me!"? That seems to be all that matters. I will admit that sometimes I am guilty of this kind of thinking.

We might walk though fire to get what we want, but won't walk across the street to ask a neighbor, "How was your day? Anything new going on with you?" We might not give up a few hours on Saturday to help an elderly person with some yard work, but can spend the entire day looking for just the right outfit to wear that night. We might impose on or inconvenience others because, "I just have to do what's best for me".

I am so thankful that Jesus isn't like this. He didn't focus on what Ee wanted or what He needed. He just said, "Father, not My will, but Yours be done!" (Luke 22:42). He loved His Father. He loved us. He gave of Himself for God's will. He did, not what was best for Him, but what was best for us!

We Live

Because I live, you will live also. – John 14:19

One hymn that comes to mind in reading this is, "Because He Lives". The words to this hymn are so comforting, "Because He lives, I can face tomorrow. Because He lives, all fear is gone. Because I know He holds the future, life is worth living just because He lives". Amazing! We have this awesome Living Savior that is with us, always!

We don't have to worry, He lives. We don't have to fear, He lives. We can face tomorrow and the future that lies ahead because He lives in us. We can have the life that He meant for us and all the blessings that come with it. We have the power of a Living God inside our hearts. All we have to do is trust it! Because He lives, we don't just exist and follow clumsily through this world – we live!

ox CRO

March 22

The Long Robe

Give, and it will be given to you. A good measure, pressed down, shaken together and running over, will be poured into your lap. For with the measure you use, it will be measured to you. - Luke 6:38

In Biblical times, a long robe was used to carry the overflow of grain. When the amount was so abundant that they could not carry it, would be "poured into their lap" in order to be transported. In other words, they were given more than they could possibly carry.

When we give ourselves, and of ourselves to Jesus, we are blessed. Psalm 23 tells us that "my cup overflows" (Psalm 23:5) and in John, Jesus tells us "I have come that they may have life, and have it abundantly" (John 10:10). Give, and it will be given to you. Are you a giving person? Well, you better get out your long robe!

March 23

Choose Him

I lay down my life.....No one takes it from Me. – John 10:17-18

I am awed by the fact that Jesus, God, perfect in every way, chose to die for sin. His sin? No, my sin – your sin. He was beaten, mocked, stripped of flesh and dignity for us. He didn't deserve what happened to Him. He chose to follow this bloody path all the way to the end. He chose this so we could be saved.

There are many things in this life that are not fair. That's life! We don't always get to have things our way. We have our own crosses to carry. We have our own path to follow. Not everything is going to be easy, but we can follow the lead of the One who gave it all for us. Make time for Him. Make choices with Him in mind. Remember, He chose you. Have you chosen Him?

ඉළ ඉ

March 24

He's Alive

He is not here, but is risen! – Matthew 28:6

Aren't you thankful you don't worship a dead guy? Aren't you glad you aren't praying to someone who can no longer hear you? Aren't you blessed because He lives? Our God is alive and well and living with us this very day. He isn't a memory cherished in books or shrines. He's not just a nice, wise man from the past that's long gone away. Our God is "The Alpha and the Omega, the Beginning and the End; Who is and Who was and Who is to come" (Revelation 1:8). He died on the cross, but that didn't stop Him. He rose on that third day to live with us and to love us forever more! Amen and Hallelujah! Sorry, got a little excited there!

Easter season is such an exciting time, and not because of eggs, or bunnies, or pictures in pretty dresses – it's because that is when our Lord proved once and again Who He is. Take time to reflect on Who He is, on what He did and is still doing for you and in you, and on just how amazing the sacrifice He made truly is. Death and the grave couldn't stop Him – He's alive!

꧁ ꧂

March 25

The One Who Knows

*Trust in the Lord with all your heart and lean not
on your own understanding. - Proverbs 3:5*

I don't always know what that right thing to do is. I don't always chose the right path for my life. I don't claim to have the gift of discernment. I can't always trust my way of thinking. These are just some of the many reasons that I need Jesus.

Paul writes in Ephesians, "In Him we have redemption through His blood, the forgiveness of sins, in accordance with the riches of God's grace that He lavished on us with all wisdom and understanding. And He made known to us the mystery of His will according to His good pleasure" (Ephesians 1:7-9). Like I said, I don't always know, but I can put my trust in the One Who does!

March 26

God's On the Case

He is my defender; I will not be defeated. – Psalm 62:6

Once, I was watching a TV show about a court case. The defense attorney kept telling his client that it was his job to fight and the client's job to trust. If the client could do this, he would go free. The client didn't listen, and kept interrupting and trying to intercede on his own behalf, only making things worse.

When we have a problem, when we are being treated unfairly, when the walls seem to be closing in, God is there. He is our defender and with Him, we will not be defeated! He will fight for us if we trust in Him. He will bring us through any hardship if we have faith in Him. I don't know about you, but I sometimes tend to interrupt Him and try to intercede on my own behalf – only making things worse. Don't be defeated; put yourself in God's hands!

March 27

Having Him

Then Jesus said to him, "Unless you people see signs and
wonders, you will by no means believe". – John 4:48

I have had people say to me that they don't believe in God because
they have seen no evidence that He exists. In Biblical times, there
were many signs and wonders. Some examples of these are when
the Red Sea parted (Exodus 14:21), when Daniel survived the lion's
den (Daniel 6:22), and when Jesus fed the five thousand (Matthew
14:19-20). These were all done and seen, but still some didn't believe.
It seems that seeing does not always believe.

Scripture tells us, "For we walk by faith, not by sight" (2 Corinthains
5:7), "The eyes of those who see will not be dim, and the ears of those
who hear will listen" (Isaiah 32:3), and "Blessed are your eyes for
they see, and your ears for they hear" (Matthew 13:16). There has to
be something to go along with your seeing and your hearing in order
to truly see and to truly hear. That something is faith!

Knowing what these Biblical miracles were means you know your
history. Believing that they happened because our living God can do
anything, means you have faith. Find this faith. If you do, you will
have faith that He can and will perform miracles for you too!

March 28

Sharing Jesus

The one who believes in the Son of God has the
testimony in himself. – 1 John 5:10

I used to think that I couldn't share my faith with others. I didn't
know what to say. I didn't think I had anything worth saying. I
was afraid of what the other person might say or what they might
think. In most cases, I just ended up not saying anything and let the
opportunity past me by.

When I don't know what to say, I need to remember, "The Holy
Spirit, whom the Father will send in my name, will teach you all
things and will remind you of everything I have said to you" (John
14:26). When I don't feel I have anything worth saying, I need to
remember, "That you yourselves are full of goodness, complete in
knowledge and competent to instruct one another" (Romans 15:14).
When I fear the reaction of others, I need to remember, "Blessed are
you when people insult you, persecute you and falsely say all kinds
of evil against you because of me" (Matthew 5:11).

Sharing Jesus with others is just about sharing what He has done
for you. Now, I tell people, "Well, let me tell you how He changed
me" or "Let me share how this relationship works for me." I can only
truly know my own experience and I can tell it. I should be able to
tell my story of faith without fear. Basically, it's just a conversation
with another person. The old hymn says, "I love to tell the story....,"
let that be true in me and in you!

Faithful in Prayer

Devote yourselves to prayer, being watchful
and thankful. – Colossians 4:2

On my way to work one morning, in the rain, a guy hydroplaned right in front of me and slammed into the bridge wall. I just knew I was going to hit him, as well as the car right beside me. I didn't slam on my brakes because I didn't want to start spinning too. I didn't swerve, because there were cars all around me. I just started slowing down and watching to see when and where he stopped. In the end, my car was just a few feet away when it slowed to a stop. I got out of my car to check on him, he hit pretty hard. He was physically fine, so I left and went to work. I called my mother to tell her what happened and she said, "Well, I was sitting here praying that you got to work okay in this weather."

I don't claim to be the best driver so I'm sure that it was my mother's prayer, not my attention to detail, that kept me safe that morning. The book of James tells us that, "the prayer of a righteous man is powerful and effective" (5:16). We need to keep each other in our prayers. When you tell someone, "You are in my prayers" or "I will pray for you," you need to mean it and actually do it. Paul states in Romans, "Be joyful in hope, patient in affliction, faithful in prayer" (12:12). Who are you praying for today? You never know when they are really going to need it!

ᗧᏇᎸᗣᎸᏇᗣ

March 30

Wake Up!

I do not understand my own actions. For I do not do what
I want, but I do the very thing I hate. - Romans 7:15

You know, God's timing is perfect. I opened my little book one
morning, and this verse was the first one I saw. I had to laugh at
myself. That morning had not been my typical morning. I woke up
late, because I had turned off my alarm, and rushed to get ready.
Then, I got in my car to go to work and my tank was on empty.
Then I remembered that the day before, on my way home, I noticed
I needed to get gas, but didn't feel like stopping then. So, here I was
late for work, trying very hard to get into a bad mood, and I read "I
do not understand my own actions." I had to smile and say, "Okay
God, you got me on this one!"

Sometimes, when life gets tough, we do it to ourselves. We don't
do what we are supposed to be doing. We don't think about the
consequences of our actions. We don't stop and think, "How is this
going to turn out?" We can stay asleep in life instead of waking up
and being responsible for our actions.

Keep God close when making decisions. Seek Him when temptation
comes knocking. Use His strength to make life easier to take. Ask
Him to be your alarm, and when it goes off, wake up!

༺ ༠༅ ༅༠ ༻

March 31

Steady on Your Feet

The Lord set my feet on a rock and gave me
a firm place to stand. - Psalm 40:2

I'm not always the most graceful person in the world. I can sometimes trip over my own feet on flat ground with tennis shoes on. Anytime I do this with others around, I will instinctively reach out for help. They, in turn, will instinctively reach out and try to grab me. They try to keep me from falling. They will also keep a grip on me until I'm steady on my feet again.

There are going to be times in this life when we tend to stumble. We can easily loose our balance and start to fall. If we will reach out to Jesus, He will, in turn, reach out and grab us. He will keep us from falling. And He will be there holding on until we are steady on our feet again!

April 1

Times of Unrest

When you lie down, you will not be afraid; you will lie down,
and your sleep will be pleasant. - Proverbs 3:24

I sometimes have trouble sleeping. There are times when I lie down and my mind can't stop racing and slow down enough for rest to come. Other times I wake up in the middle of the night and start thinking about different things and can't manage to fall back to sleep. Either way, the next day isn't much fun.

The things that might keep me up at night can differ. It might be something I'm upset about, or worried about, or angry about. It can be the anticipation of something that's unclear. In those times of restlessness, if I would just continually remind myself to let go and trust God, I believe that peace would wash over me and sleep would come. In times of worry and unrest, let go and trust in Him. Always remember that "weeping may endure for a night, but joy comes in the morning" (Psalm 30:5)!

ೲഇ ഇൕ

April 2

Carrying Our Cross

As they were going out, they met a man from Cyrene, named
Simon, and they forced him to carry the cross. - Matthew 27:32

The picture this passage of scripture paints is a humble reminder of
what our sin did to Jesus. The beating Jesus went through before
even walking up the hill to Golgotha made Him too weak to carry
His own cross. A man named Simon came out of the crowd and
helped him carry it the rest of the way. This shows that while human,
He had our weaknesses. All except one, He had no sin!

In reading this passage, I thought of Jesus' words, "If anyone would
come after me, he must deny himself and take up his cross and
follow me" (Matthew 16:24). We have to carry our cross, but we
don't have to do it alone. He is with us. Because of us, Jesus needed
help carrying His cross. Knowing that, why would we ever think we
could carry ours alone?

April 3

Stay Close to Him

When you draw close to God, God will draw close to you. – James 4:8

Have you ever tried to hug someone that doesn't hug you back? This doesn't work well. Have you ever tried to have a conversation with someone who isn't paying attention to a word you are saying? This can be frustrating. Have you ever tried to have a relationship with someone who just isn't interested in you? This can be heartbreaking. In order to be close to someone, they have to want to be close to you. It is the same in your relationship with God.

You can't feel God's embrace if you are always holding Him at an arm's length. You can't hear His still small voice if you are too busy to listen. You can't have a relationship with Him unless you want one because He will not force Himself into your life. But, "when you draw close to God, God will draw close to you!"

April 4

Stand for the Truth

Most assuredly, I say to you, he who does not enter the
sheepfold by the door, but climbs up some other way,
the same is a thief and a robber. – John 10:1

We live in a confusing age. By the world's view, everything is okay,
believe what you want, do what you want, and there are many ways
to Heaven. Tolerance of everything is on the rise. I saw a quote once
that said, "If you don't stand for something, you'll fall for anything."
We are seeing proof of this statement all over the world.

The Bible tells us that "there is one body and one Spirit, just as you
were called to one hope when you were called, one Lord, one faith,
one baptism; one God and Father of all, who is over all and through
all and in all" (Ephesians 4:4-6). It also tells us the words of Jesus, "I
am the way and the truth and the life. No one comes to the Father
except through me" (John 14:6). There is no other way! There is no
other truth! So, you can stand for the truth or fall for the lie!

April 5

Obeying God's Will

Father, if you are willing, take this cup from me; yet
not my will, but yours be done. – Luke 22:42

Easter is not only a celebration of Christ's resurrection; it's a lesson in obedience. There are so many things to reflect on during this season. Christ sacrifice for our sins. The brutal punishment He went through as an innocent man. His cruel and painful death. Then, His resurrection, just as He said it would happen. All of this happened because of His obedience to His father. He didn't want to suffer, but He did. He wished that there was another way, but there wasn't. In the end, "not my will, but yours be done" was His purpose and action. Paul writes in Philppians, "He humbled Himself and became obedient to the point of death, even the death of the cross" (Philippians 2:8). And because of this, you and I can be saved by grace through faith and have eternal life.

We learn many things by studying the Word of God and the actions of Christ. We learn to love without judgment. We learn to have compassion on the weak and suffering. We learn to give rather that to receive. We also learn that it's not always about what we want, but what God's will is. Obedience, let's give it a try!

April 6

My Father's Blessing

And his father Isaac said to him, "Who are you?" So he said,
"I am your son, your firstborn, Esau." – Genesis 27:32

In this story from Genesis, Jacob and Esau were brothers. Jacob had earlier stolen Esau's birthright (as firstborn son) from him. Now, Jacob also wanted Esau's blessing from their old and blind father. In ancient Biblical times, a blessing was always given to sons at the end of the father's life, the blessing of the first born being most significant. With the help of their mother, Rebekah, Jacob decided to disguise himself as Esau. So when Isaac thought he was giving this most sacred of blessings to Esau, he mistakenly gave it to Jacob instead.

Don't we sometimes pretend to be someone else in order to get what we want? We can often fool those around us, even those closest to us. We can even fool ourselves. There is One whom we cannot fool and that is God. He knows us. He knows our intentions and our goals. He knows our fears and our dreams. He knows who we really are.

When we come to God, and put our faith and trust in Him, we receive His blessings - the blessings that were meant for us. We don't have to be someone else. We don't have to pretend. We don't have to scheme. We don't have to wear a disguise. We can just be ourselves. Isn't that a comfort?

April 7

The Best Table

For who is greater, he who sits at the table, or he who
serves? Is it not he who sits at the table? Yet I am
among you as the One who serves. – Luke 22:27

When I was in kindergarten, the kids in my classroom would fight
over one table. We would race to get there first and even push
someone out of a seat in order to sit at this special table. I can't even
remember now what was so exciting about this table, but even as five
year olds, we felt the need to sit at the best table.

We all sometimes feel entitled to sit at the best table. But, do we ever
race to be the one who serves? Do we ever want to be the one running
around doing all the work while others get to look important, getting
pampered and spoiled? Jesus said, "The Son of Man did not come to
be served, but to serve" (Matthew 20:28). We don't need to spend
our time fighting for the best table, we need to do good, help others,
spread God's Word, and hopefully one day hear Jesus say, "Well
done, good and faithful servant" (Matthew 25:21), followed by "you
may eat and drink at My table in My kingdom" (Luke 22:30). Now,
to me, that would be the best table!

Just Believe

"Assuredly, I say to you, today you will be
with Me in Paradise." - Luke 23:43

The man that Jesus said these words to was not a disciple. It was not a man that had followed Him from city to city spreading His gospel. He was not a man who had built churches or helped the elderly, children, and widows. He was not a man that this world would consider a "good" person. He was a criminal, dying on a cross beside our Savior. Why did Jesus say these words to Him? Because this criminal said, "Jesus, remember me when you come into your kingdom" (Luke 23:42). He believed, he asked, and he was with Jesus that day in Paradise.

Anyone can come to Jesus. Anyone can be welcomed into His kingdom. "For God so loved the world that He gave His only son, that whoever believes in Him, shall not perish but have everlasting life" (John 3:16). This verse only mentions one action from us that matters. It doesn't mater what you did. It doesn't matter what you didn't do. What does matter is what you have to do......just believe!

⸙⸙⸙

April 9

It's Possible

With God nothing will be impossible. - Luke 1:37

We say a lot of things are impossible. Saving your marriage. Fighting an illness. Finding a job. We even use the "impossible" word for simpler things like losing weight, getting your child to mind, saving money or even finding enough time in the day. We like to use impossible because we think it allows us to just give up. But......

With God nothing is impossible. You can start communicating with your spouse without the bitter resentments you've let build up. You can have the strength to carry on even when your body says otherwise. You can find opportunities through a door you didn't notice was open. Jesus said, "With man this is impossible, but with God all things are possible" (Matthew 19:26). When you find yourself face to face with the impossible, seek the One Who has no impossible!

April 10

Eternal Praising

There will be no more death, sadness, crying, or pain,
because all the old ways are gone. - Revelation 21:4

Two of my friend lost their grandmothers in the same week. These two sweet grandmothers that had been very sick the last few months of their lives. They were so sick that their families had a hard time watching them suffer. After the watching and waiting finally ended, these two ladies went home to meet Jesus, and started singing praises to their Lord forever and forever. What a blessing this is for a believer and what a comfort it is for the families they leave behind!

Death comes in this life, but isn't an end. As Christians, we go on to live with Jesus forever. In Heaven, "there will be no more death, sadness, crying, or pain", just eternal praising, "Holy, Holy, Holy is the Lord God Almighty" (Revelation 4:8).

ৰৌৎ ৎৰৎ

April 11

God's Grace

If they could be made God's people by what they did, God's
gift of grace would not really be a gift. - Romans 11:6

When someone gives you a birthday gift, do you open it and say,
"This is great! How much do I owe you?" I hope not. You open it,
say thank you, and enjoy it because it was given by someone else to
you. Gifts are free. You don't have to earn them!

I say that "blessings are sometimes called gifts because they don't
cost you anything." God's gift of grace is a blessing. Something you
get by just accepting it. The only cost was not to you. It was to Jesus
who paid for it on a cross, so many years ago!

இ12 ௬௯

April 12

Faith, Hope, and Love

And now abide faith, hope, love, these three; but the
greatest of these is love. – 1 Corinthians 13:13

"Faith, hope, and love – these three." Of faith Jesus would ask, "Why
are you fearful, O you of little faith?" or "Why did you doubt?"
(Matthew 8:26, 14:31). He also said to some, "Rise and go; your
faith has made you well" (Luke 17:19). Faith in God leads us to
hope in His promises, "Let Your mercy, O Lord, be upon us, just as
we hope in You" (Psalm 33:22); "Now hope does not disappoint"
(Romans 5:5); "May the God of hope fill you" (Romans 15:13), and
"This hope (in God's truth) we have as an anchor of the soul, both
sure and steadfast" (Hebrews 6:19). And finally, "but the greatest
of these is love," there are way too many verses of scripture on love
to put them in this hopefully short devotional – but there is one I
wanted to mention, "For God so loved the world that He gave His
only son, so whoever believes in Him, shall not perish, but have
everlasting life" (John 3:16). To me, this is the greatest testament of
love in all of scripture!

Faith, hope, and love are all sometimes hard to accomplish. Faith
means you have to believe in something. Hope means you have to
lean on or depend on something. Loves means you have to give of
yourself to something. Can you think of a better "something" that
our Savior, Jesus Christ?

April 13

Leap of Faith

We may boldly say, "The Lord is my helper; I
will not be afraid." - Hebrews 13:6

When my nieces were little, and they wanted to jump off the diving
board, I would have to get out in the middle of the swimming pool,
tread water, and catch them when they jumped in. They would
leap off that diving board with their arms held out, trusting that I
would be there to catch them. Trusting that I would keep them from
sinking and get them safely back to steady ground.

We have to make giant leaps of faith in this life. We are often
jumping into unfamiliar waters not knowing where it will lead. God
asks that we trust in Him. God may be calling you or urging you to
do something that seems scary to you, uncertainty may be haunting
you, or you just might be plain scared. Just as Peter literally stepped
out of the boat, we have to do the same. If we trust that He is there
to catch us, keep us from sinking, and get us safely on our feet!

April 14

Imitators of God

Be imitators of God, therefore, as dearly
loved children. - Ephesians 5:1

One night I was visiting a friend of mine. Her two year old daughter, Claudia, was there with us. As I was talking, I noticed Claudia was imitating me. At one time, I was resting my head between my index finger and my thumb, with my head tilted a little bit. As I watched her, she was trying to get her fingers in the same position and tilting her head exactly like mine. Later, I was telling a story and using my hands as I talked, I looked over at Claudia and she was moving her mouth, nodding, and waving her hands around. She was trying to do everything I was doing. It's a good thing I was on my best behavior!

As Christians, we are to be imitators of God. One Bible commentary puts it like this, "The Christian life is designed to reproduce godliness as modeled by the Savior and Lord, Jesus Christ". We are to act how He acted, love as He loved, and serve as He served. Just as Claudia couldn't have imitated me without first studying my actions, we can't be like Christ without studying His life!

April 15

Death and Taxes

Render therefore to Caesar the things that
are Caesar's. – Matthew 22:21

April 15th, tax day. There is a saying I've heard people use, "There are two sure things in life – death and taxes." This is true, but they are leaving out one other sure thing and that is Jesus Christ! There are many things in this life that disappoint, fade away, and can't be relied upon. I'm so glad that my Savior and Lord Jesus Christ is none of those things! He is always there. He knows exactly what I need when I need it and knows the answers to all my questions.

Remember, in this uncertain life, look to Jesus. Lean on Him. Depend on Him. Know that through Him, anything is possible. And if you have to write a big check today, also remember these words of Jesus, "Blessed are the poor" (of course, this is taken a little out of context here, for the true message read Matthew 5 – The Sermon on the Mount)! I guess my thought today is, "Wouldn't it be nice to have more assurance in life than death and taxes?"

April 16

Which Character Are You?

The Son of Man must suffer many things, and be rejected
by the elders and chief priests and scribes, and be
killed, and be raised the third day. – Luke 9:22

In looking at the Easter message, I am always how amazing my God is. It is also a reminder that His will is going to happen. Jesus knew when He came what was going to happen to Him. He knew His purpose and how this story would play out. Who didn't know? The other characters in the story. Shakespeare said, "The whole world's a stage, and the men and women merely players." In any play, there are good guys and bad guys. In Jesus' story, the same holds true. The scribes and Pharisees didn't know they would be responsible for killing the Messiah, because they could only selfishly see their power diminishing. Judas didn't know he would be the betrayer of the Christ, because he could only see his greed. The disciples didn't know they were being groomed to spread the gospel to the world, because they were only following what was in their heart. Scripture was being fulfilled in front of their very eyes and they were just living their lives.

God's will continues today and there are different sides, just as in Jesus' day. Are you going to be a "good guy" or a "bad guy?" Are you going to be a pawn in Satan's game, totally dispensable to him? Or are you going to be one of the saints that go marching in for Jesus, while He hold you close like a shepherd guarding His sheep? Scripture tells us, "Either make the tree good and its fruit good, or else make the tree bad and its fruit bad, for a tree is known by its fruit" (Matthew 12:33). The scribes and Pharisees are known for killing Jesus. Judas Iscariot is known for betraying Jesus. The disciples are known as faithful followers of Jesus. What will you be known for? You have a purpose in His will. Think about it today, which character are you?

April 17

Helpless Sheep

And Jesus, when He came out, saw a great multitude
and was moved with compassion for them, because they
were like sheep not having a shepherd. – Mark 6:34

Sheep are known to be helpless. That is why they need constant care. They are prone to wonder off and will stumble into danger without knowing it. They can get turned upside down with no way of getting themselves right side up. Do you ever wonder why we are compared to sheep so much in scripture? Don't we do the same thing?

I am definitely a helpless sheep and I have wondered from familiar surroundings. I have stumbled into danger and sometimes I've dove in head first. I know all too well what it's like to have a life that is turned upside down, with no clue how to make it right. That is why I am so thankful for my Shepherd. Jesus said, "I am the Good Shepherd; and I know My sheep, and am known by My own" (John 10:14). Jesus can make my path straight. He can shine a light in my darkness. He can make my upside down, right side up again!

ೋೋ ೋ

April 18

Boldly Sharing

Assuredly, I say to you, among those born of women, there has
not risen one greater than John the Baptist. - Matthew 11:11

John the Baptist was known as a fearless and bold spokesman for
God. It had been over 400 years since Malachi's final prophetic
words that a messenger was to come and announce the arrival of
the Messiah (Malachi 4:5). John the Baptist was that messenger.
His message was certainly clear, the promised Messiah was about
to come, and those listening must repent of their sins. He wasn't
afraid of what people thought. He wasn't silent in front of those
who disagreed with him. He had a large following, drawn to his
message.

One lesson to be learned from John the Baptist is that God will
give you the courage you need. He was bold in his faith and in the
sharing of his faith. It didn't matter to him if people responded
negatively to his message. He had a purpose and intended to fulfill
it. So, that co-worker you had wanted to share your testimony with,
do it! That family member that you want to share your concern for,
do it! That friend you're afraid you will lose if you share the gospel
with them, just do it! Ask Jesus for the courage and boldness to share
His gospel with others and He will give it to you!

April 19

Benefits of Forgiveness

Make allowance for each other's faults, and forgive
anyone who offends you. Remember, the Lord forgave
you, so you must forgive others. – Colossians 3:13

When we are offended or hurt by another, it can lead to unforgiveness.
Unforgorgiveness can lead to anger, bitterness, and ultimately to
resentment. Resentment can lead to hate and hate can lead to a
hardened heart.

I believe forgiveness is not only an act of obedience and discipline
that God commands us to do, but it's an action that can keep our
hearts alive. Have you ever seen an angry person happy for long?
Have you ever seen someone who can't forgive a certain person or
event ever get past it? Forgiveness has two sided benefits. Sure, it
helps the person receiving the forgiveness, but based on my own
experience, it helps the forgiver just as much or more!

ɔ৫ ৯ɔ₀

April 20

The Street Preacher

*Son of man, I have made you a watchman for the
house of Israel; therefore hear a word from My mouth,
and give them warning from Me. - Ezekiel 3:17*

Ezekiel, one of the Old Testament prophets, was sometimes called a "street preacher." The Israelites were in exile, controlled by the Babylonians. There were no temple pulpits to preach from and no tent revivals that drew major crowds. He had to go to the people. He had to hit the streets because he had a message to deliver. God had called him to be a watchman for his people. He had a responsibility to tell the people about God, about the need to repent of their sins, and the consequences of their disobedience.

We, as Christians, have a responsibility to tell others about Jesus. Those who are lost usually don't just show up at a church without first getting an invitation. Take a lesson from this "street preacher," they are not going to come to us; we need to go to them!

April 21

Expectations and Acceptance

The Lord does not look at the things man looks
at. Man looks at the outward appearance, but the
Lord looks at the heart. – 1 Samuel 16:7

Do you ever feel like you can't please anyone? We put impossible expectations on ourselves, our friends, our coworkers, our children, and our spouses. In this world, we often need to fit into a certain "package" in order to be accepted. We have heard others say things like, "She isn't pretty enough", "He doesn't make very much money", "She's doesn't have enough education", or "Did you hear what he did?" We all have heard the reasons why we don't fit into someone else's mold of what they think we should be.

Jesus loves us just as we are. He forgets the past, helps with our present, and guides us into our future. We don't have to be anything but willing to live for Him. Have you ever thought about the fact that Jesus, who is perfect in every way, wants our acceptance and not the other way around?

April 22

False Fulfillments

Blessed are those who hunger and thirst for
righteousness, for they will be filled. – Matthew 5:6

There are so many things in this world that leave us empty. We might search for fulfillment through money, food, alcohol, drugs, power, or sex. These things will never leave us full for long. Soon you become empty again and have to go back for more. We fall in love with these false fulfillments. The sad thing is these things cannot ever return that love.

When we go to Jesus we will be filled with something that sustains. We will be filled with something that doesn't just dull, numb, or just help us to avoid, but actually does make things better. We will be filled with something real. Another amazing thing about it, when you fall in love with Jesus, that love is returned!

April 23

A Healthy Heart

*Above all else, guard your heart, for it is the
wellspring of life. – Proverbs 4:22-24*

Our heart is physically and emotionally the center of our life. If your heart isn't beating physically, you cease to live. If your heart isn't beating emotionally, you will have the same results. You might still be breathing, but you aren't living. We are taught by society how to physically take care of our heart. There are medications, exercise, stress relievers, and diets that we can learn about. The physical heart has many helpers, but the emotional heart has only one fail-proof helper and that is Jesus.

If your heart tends to worry, Jesus can comfort you. If your heart tends to be depressed, Jesus can lift you up. If your heart tends to feel alone, Jesus is always there. Whatever your heart is feeling, Jesus has the remedy ready and waiting. A healthy heart is essential to live a healthy life. Put your heart under the care of the Great Physician! You won't need a second opinion!

ↄ℮℧ ℧℮ↄ

April 24

God's Grace

But to each one of us grace has been given as
Christ apportioned it. - Ephesians 4:7

I have a tendency to look back on past mistakes and let myself dwell on them. I try not to and am getting better, but Satan knows what he's doing. He knows how to get to me and he does a great job of catching me off guard. I can have those moments when I think, "I don't deserve God's grace or mercy, look what I've done in my life". Satan is always there to reply, "No you don't, so quit thinking God's actually going to give it to you!"

In studying this verse, my Bible Commentary explains it like this, "Grace is a single-word definition of the gospel". I love that. God chooses to give his grace to us because of love, His love. His love and grace are unmerited, unearned, and undeserved - and that's okay. Once, when I was having one of the moments I mentioned above, a dear friend looked at me, gave me her sweet smile, and said, "Why can't you just accept God's grace and move on?" If you tend to have these moments like mine, I'll ask that same question to you.

◦๑ ๑◦

April 25

A Heart for Him

Create in me a new heart, O God. – Psalm 51:10

I am always amazed when I read the words of David. He was not a perfect person, not by a long shot. What he did, that so many people miss, was repent of his sins. He didn't shift blame to someone else. He didn't say, "what if?" He didn't avoid the things he had done. He said, "I'm sorry." He stayed close to God and wanted God to stay close to him. He truly longed to be the man God wanted him to be and in his longing he said the words, "Create in me a new heart, O God". Because of this attitude, David is remembered in scripture as "a man after God's own heart" (1 Samuel 13:14).

Most of us never want to admit fault. We don't like to be wrong or blamed for anything. We don't like to be the one who messed up. These feelings are normal, but that doesn't mean our mistakes didn't happen. Like with David, God knows our faults and shortcomings. He knows we aren't perfect and loves us anyway. Ask God to create a new heart in you. Ask Him to create a heart that longs for closeness with Him and longs to be like Him. I know we don't like to be wrong, so let's not miss the way to be right!

April 26

Lifting When Heavy

But commission Joshua, and encourage and strengthen him,
for he will lead this people across and will cause them to
inherit the land that you will see. – Deuteronomy 3:28

It is very hard to encourage someone who is getting what you want. This is exactly what God asked Moses to do for Joshua. With God's divine help, Moses was the one who brought the Israelites out of their bondage in Egypt and was the one who led them across the wilderness and listened night and day to their complaining. He was the one who gave them the commandments and their rules for living. He was the one trying to get them to the Promised Land – but, he would never get there. Joshua, not Moses, would be the one to cross over into the "land flowing with milk and honey" (Exodus 3:8). In the end, Moses called for Joshua, and as all Israel watched, he said to him, "Be strong and courageous! For you will lead these people into the land that the Lord swore to their ancestors he would give them. Do not be afraid or discouraged, for the Lord will personally go ahead of you. He will be with you; he will neither fail you nor abandon you" (Deuteronomy 31:7-8).

Wow! Moses is a bigger person than some of us might be. Sometimes we work hard for something or pray for something, and it seems that somebody else is always getting what we want. Happy marriages, healthy babies, big promotions, financial security, trusting friendships, and good personal health – this list could go on. We need to follow the lead of Moses and look into the eyes of those people and be an encourager, be happy for them. Remind them that "He will be with you; he will neither fail you nor abandon you." Lifting someone else up, encouraging them, praying for their continued blessings, all the while having a heavy heart, can this be done? It can, but it isn't easy. My prayer today is that God help me learn this kind of unselfishness and practice it daily in my life!

ᴥᴥᴥ

April 27

Solid Food

Anyone who lives on milk, being still an infant, is not acquainted
with the teaching about righteousness. - Hebrews 5:13

Once, our pastor preached on the above verse. I got to thinking
about my family and friends with young children. Now a days,
there is a certain age when you can feed them this or that. They
have formula or their mother's milk until they are at least a year
old. In food, cereal comes first, then baby food, then "real people"
food. Depending on the mother, some follow it sternly, some more
laid back. The point is that these children progress, move forward
on the food pyramid, come to need something other than milk, and
move on to solid food.

Paul finished the above verse with, "But solid food is for the mature,
who by constant use have trained themselves to distinguish well
from evil" (Hebrews 5:114). Just as children progress to solid food,
as Christians, so should we. An infant in Christ only needs to know
that God loves them, that Jesus died for them, and that if they
believe in that - they will live forever with Him. As we mature, we
have to move on from what Christ did for us to what we should be
doing for Him and for others. It's not all about us anymore!

Just as we grow physically, we need to also grow spiritually. Don't
stay a spiritual infant, study God's Word, find out His will for your
life, and move on to solid food!

Don't Expect Something Else

John sent them to the Lord to ask, "Are you the one who was
to come, or should we expect someone else?" – Luke 7:19

John the Baptist sent men to ask Jesus if he was the awaited Messiah.
When they asked Jesus this question, He replied, "Go back and
report to John what you have seen and heard: The blind receive sight,
the lame walk, those who have leprosy are cured, the deaf hear, the
dead are raised, and the good news is preached to the poor." John
the Baptist heard this and believed!

So many in Jesus' day did not believe He was the Messiah. They
feared Him, not in reverence, but in selfishness. They resented Him,
because He was not what they pictured God's Son to be. They
questioned Him, because they did not and could not understand.
It didn't matter what He said or did, they would not believe. He
was what they had waited for, but they decided to "expect someone
else".

Jesus gives us countless blessings in this life. He paid the ultimate
sacrifice so we could have eternal life with Him. He loves us
unconditionally. We need to believe as John the Baptist believed.
Don't expect someone else, hear Him, see Him for who He is, and
believe!

All Understanding

And the peace of God, which transcends all understanding, will guard your hearts and your minds in Christ Jesus. - Philippians 4:7

When I read this verse, I thought of how perfect it is. The part that talks about "which transcends all understanding" really got to me. This is why someone suffering from a fatal illness is peaceful instead of bitter, why someone's death can be a cause for happiness instead of sorrow, and why someone dealing with a serious problem can still smile and say "I know it will be alright".

As Christians, we can have peace that others don't understand. We can go through difficult times and they won't change who we are inside. We have "the peace of God, which transcends all understanding and it will guard our hearts and our minds in Christ Jesus"!

Notice Him

Blessed are your eyes because they see, and your
ears because they hear. - Matthew 13:16

Have you ever been looking for your sunglasses and find them
perched on your head? Have you ever been searching for your keys
and realized that you were already holding them in your hand? It's
sad to admit, but I've done both of these. I get to rushing around,
not paying full attention to what I'm doing, and things get missed.
Things that I'm so use to being there that I no longer notice them.

Sometimes, I feel like we let this happen to our relationship with
Jesus. We search for answers, and He's waiting, ready to give them.
We need peace and comfort, and He's waiting, ready to embrace
us. We reach out, not realizing that He's already holding our hand.
Don't get so used to Him being there that you no longer notice
Him!

May 1

The Path of Unforgiveness

If you do not forgive men their trespasses, neither will
your Father forgive your trespasses. - Matthew 6:15

I have often thought that the path of unforgiveness can lead to a
sad life. It is not only for the person who needs the forgiveness, but
for the one who can't give it. It's very hard to forgive someone who
has hurt you, harmed you, or damaged you in some way. Keeping
your mind and heart occupied with all those you are angry with,
keeps your mind and heart from being filled with other things like
love, joy, and peace.

Scripture tells us that if we do not forgive others, we will not be
forgiven. It really doesn't get any plainer than that. The reason I
think unforgiveness can lead to a sad life is that it keeps you from
being close to Jesus. Your inability to forgive can put a barrier up
between you and Him. Anger doesn't see anything but anger. Let
it go and see Jesus!

꧁ ꧂

May 2

Pass the Test

In all your getting, get understanding. - Proverbs 4:7

Anyone who is or has been in school knows that you will do better on a test if you studied. Believe me, I tried it the other way around! Usually, the more you studied, the better you performed. The more time you spent on a subject, the more familiar you were with it. Ultimately, you understood it better.

The same principal applies to God's Word. How are you supposed to know what it says if you have never read it? How are you supposed to know what to do unless you've read its instructions? The answers to the tests we face daily are in its pages. Don't you want to pass?

Anything in the World

"Give me wisdom and knowledge, that I may
lead this people." - 2 Chronicles 1:10

I am always amazed when I read the story of Solomon. We have all played the game, "If you could have anything in the world, what would it be?" Common answers are usually, money, beauty, happiness, and as I get older, health is a common answer. Solomon wasn't playing a game. Unselfishly, he was asking God for what he thought he needed when he said, "Give me wisdom and knowledge, that I may lead this people" (2 Chronicles 1:10). God answered him, "Since this is your heart's desire and you have not asked for wealth, riches or honor, not for the death of your enemies, and since you have not asked for a long life but for wisdom and knowledge to govern My people over whom I have made you king, therefore wisdom and knowledge will be given to you. And I will also give you wealth, riches and honor, such as no king who was before you had and none after you will have" (2 Chronicles 11-12). Wow!

To me, the story of Solomon asking for wisdom, is an excellent example of "No eye has seen, no ear has heard, no mind has conceived what God has prepared for those who love him" (1 Corinthians 2:9). Solomon wasn't thinking of himself, he just wanted the tools to be the best king for God's people that he could be. He wasn't self seeking, but seeking God's will. In doing this, he was blessed beyond measure. So, the next time you're playing, "If you could have anything in the world, what would it be?" - put some extra thought into your answer!

ౌ௸ ௸ౌ

May 4

Needing Others

Two are better than one, because they have a good
reward for their labor. For if they fall, one will lift up his
companion. But woe to him who is alone when he falls, for
he has no one to help him up. - Ecclesiastes 4:9-10

One night, when I was right in the middle of doing laundry, the light bulb in my laundry room went out. Instead of waiting for someone to be there to help me, I decided to change it right then and finish what I was doing. The ceiling in my laundry room is really high, so I got out a ladder, climbed up with one hand, the flash light in the other hand and the light bulb secured between my teeth. Should I have called a friend or a neighbor to help me? Probably. Should I have waited for help instead of being impatient and doing this task right then? Sure. Should I have waited for a steady hand on that ladder instead of climbing up on the wobbly thing alone? Definitely! If I had fallen, there would have been no one there to catch me.

There have been moments in my life when I needed someone to catch me. I've fallen so hard that I wouldn't have gotten up without the help of Jesus and those He had placed in my life. Through Him and through them, I was picked up, brushed off, and led to stable ground. I can also feel the steady hands that daily keep me grounded. God blesses us with friends and family for a reason. We are made for companionship. We are given arms to hug, hands to reach out, and hearts to care. Don't think you have to go through this life alone. Remember that, when you fall (and you will), it would be nice to know that someone will be there to catch you!

.ૐ ୭ ୬.

May 5

Wandering Sheep

Your rod and your staff, they comfort me. - Psalm 23:4

The shepherd's rod and staff, also called the club and crook, were used to lead the sheep along the right path. A gentle nudge with these instruments would guide with comfort, but did not push and startle. There were used not only for direction, but for the protection of the wandering sheep. There were dangers facing the sheep that wandered away from their shepherd.

Jesus uses loving guidance when leading us along our path. He uses His rod and staff to nudge us in the right direction. Follow His path. Don't stand stubbornly when you feel Him guiding you. Don't be a wandering sheep saying, "I'd rather go this way!" Remember, His prodding is not only for direction, but for protection as well!

Ready for a Fight

Jesus said, "You have come out with swords and
clubs to capture me?" - Matthew 26:55

A large crowd with swords and clubs had been sent by the chief priests and elders to arrest Jesus. These people came ready for a fight. But, there wasn't one. Jesus went quietly. He knew what had to be done, and let it happen. I've read this story many times over the years, but have never looked at it and how it resembles some of the actions in my own life.

There are moments when I come to Jesus ready for a fight. The old "my will, His will" struggle. I really want what I want, so therefore, I'm sometimes ready to argue, or pout, or get angry when talking to Him about it. When my will doesn't coincide with His will, it isn't Him picking a fight with me, it's His way of showing me that I don't always know what's best, and that I can't see the whole picture. Don't come ready for a fight, just trust in His will and His way!

Lessons from Jonah

The Lord said, "You have been concerned about this vine,
but Nineveh has more than a hundred and twenty thousand
people who cannot tell their right hand from their left. Should
I not be concerned about that great city?" - Jonah 4:10

I love the story of Jonah, who is sometimes called the "Unwilling Prophet". Just a quick recap: Jonah was given a message from God, but didn't want to relay it to the people of Nineveh. He tried to flee from his calling, and was swallowed by a big fish. After spending three days and nights in this fish, God delivered Jonah and he was given a second chance to give God's message of judgment to the people of Nineveh. These people were warned, turned away from their sin, and God spared them. Jonah got mad when God didn't punish them as His original message had been. Then, Jonah ran off to pout and God provided a vine to shade him and ease his discomfort. Then the vine died and Jonah said he wanted to die as well. It just makes me laugh, but I won't be too hard on Jonah, because I sometimes do the same thing.

Aren't we more than happy to accept God's grace and mercy when it pertains to us? Don't we sometimes wait for others to be punished for their bad behavior while ignoring our own? Don't we sometimes focus more on the small things in life and lose sight of what's important? Let's learn from Jonah - God's grace and mercy is available for all you ask for it, God gives second chances, and God loves everyone!

May 8

His Choice

"O unbelieving and perverse generation," Jesus
replied, "how long shall I stay with you? How long
shall I put up with you?" - Matthew 17:17

Sometimes I think in amazement about the love of Jesus. I don't even think my mind can truly understand what He went through for me. His brutal death was His choice. Saving me was His choice. I was His choice.

There are lots of times when we look at those around us and think, "What are they thinking?" or "what do they think they are doing?" Jesus said the same of those around Him, "How long shall I put up with you?" He wasn't under the impression that He was dying for the righteous or the perfect or the strong. He knew exactly what He was doing and who He was doing it for. For me and for you. We were His choice!

ෙ෨෨෨ෙ

May 9

Rest for the Weary

Be merciful to me, LORD, for I am faint; O LORD, heal
me, for my bones are in agony. - Psalms 6:2

In this verse of scripture, the Psalmist is calling out to the Lord to
help his agony - both emotional and physical. When we have burdens
in our lives, it can cause physical pain. Sometimes our stomachs will
hurt. We can feel tired all the time. Stress can cause our muscles
to ache and our heads to hurt. Anxiety makes some people feel like
they are having a heart attack. There are definite signs that confirm
that our emotional state affects our physical health. You know what
can help with both of these? Spiritual strength!

Jesus said, "Come to me, all you who are weary and burdened, and
I will give you rest" (Matthew 11:28). Jesus knows of your burdens;
let Him lighten your load. Jesus knows of your hurts; let Him ease
your suffering. Jesus knows of your stresses; let Him calm your fears.
There is rest for the weary and it's Jesus! His spiritual strength will
help your emotional state and your physical well being!

May 10

Laboring in Vain

Unless the Lord builds the house, they labor
in vain who built it. - Psalm 127:1

Have you ever talked with a couple who just can't understand where they went wrong in their relationship? Have you ever seen someone who thought their new job would make everything better, only to see them later more miserable than before? Have you ever made a decision and come to realize that it wasn't the best choice?

Our success rate with our choices is much better when we start by seeking Jesus. Building the foundations of our life on Him keeps everything from crashing down around us. Praying for His guidance when making decisions, both big and small, keeps us from saying, "Well, I wish I hadn't done that!" Keeping Him close helps making the right choices easier to do. Life is sometimes hard work, so don't be one of those who labor in vain!

Don't Miss the Boat

But Noah found favor in the eyes of the Lord. - Genesis 6:8

In the days of Noah, mankind had become so bad that God said "for I am grieved that I have made them" (Genesis 6:7). But, then it goes on the say, "But Noah found favor in the eyes of the Lord." Can you imagine? Of all the people in the world, Noah was chosen to be saved. Noah wasn't righteous because he knew disaster was coming and thought he better straighten up, not because he was practicing for some unknown contest, or not because he wanted to be different in a world gone wrong. He was righteous because it was truly who he was - and God knew it!

It probably wasn't easy for Noah to stay faithful in a world so depraved that God decided to destroy it. It probably wasn't easy to stay faithful while spending 120 years building a boat so big that he couldn't conceal what he was doing. It probably wasn't easy to stay faithful while spending over a year living in close quarters with all kinds of animals. But, Noah remained faithful and true through all of his test and trials.

It's who we are, because of Who's we are, that gets us through life's test and trials. Without it, I assume Noah would have missed the boat and so will we!

༄ᶜᵉ ᵍᵉ༄

May 12

Good or Evil?

*Do not be conquered by evil, but conquer
evil with good. - Romans 12:21*

Since childhood, we have loved stories where good conquers evil. In Star Wars, the Jedi underdog bests the evil Empire. In Cinderella, the humble beauty gets the happily ever after over her selfish step-sisters. In Harry Potter, the hero is willing to sacrifice himself to save the world. As you know, I could go on here, but you get the point. There are always going to be stories were good is battling it out with evil. Why? I think it's because we can relate with this kind of struggle, because it's in our lives everyday. Why are we prone to cheer on the good guy? Not just because it's the right thing to do, but I think it's partly because we hope to get a reminder that good can win out.

We don't need fictional stories to show us that good can conquer evil. We can get all the proof we need by reading God's Word. This is the biggest battle between good and evil this world will ever see. And we already know who wins! Jesus said, "I have overcome the world" (John 16:33). Jesus has already beaten evil with His death on the cross. This battle is finished in the book of Revelation when John writes, "And the devil, who deceived them, was thrown into the lake of burning sulfur, where the beast and the false prophet had been thrown. They will be tormented day and night for ever and ever" (Revelation 20:10).

Our lives are a daily struggle between good and evil. This battle is played out in our decisions, in our actions, and in our choices everyday. If you are like me, there are going to be victory marks for both sides. But, in the end, who will win the battle for your life? Good or evil?

୭ୡ ୭ୡ

May 13

Listen and Share

But the Helper, the Holy Spirit, whom the Father will send
in My name, He will teach you all things, and bring to your
remembrance all things that I said to you. - John 14:26

While I was preparing to give my testimony to a youth group, I was completely stressed out by it. I had never done anything like this before. It wasn't just because I was about to share some of the worst things I had ever done with a group of young strangers, but I was terrified that I was going to say the wrong thing and ruin them forever! First, I had to get over myself and realize that some of them, I'm sure, weren't even going to be listening to me. Second, I had to realize that for the ones that were listening, I was just a vessel being used by the Holy Spirit and the more important work was going to be done in the hearts of those kids before I even got there and would continue long after I'd be gone. As a friend of mine said at the time, "Leigh Ann, relax and let the Holy Spirit do the heavy lifting. That's what He does."

We all worry about what to say when witnessing to a lost person, sharing our testimony with a stranger, or comforting the hurting. What we have to realize is that if we let go and listen to the Holy Spirit, He will "bring to your remembrance all things," and that's all you'll ever need!

Actions Speak

Let my prayer be set forth before Thee as incense; and the lifting up of my hands as an evening sacrifice. - Psalm 141:2

We have all heard the saying, "Actions speak louder than words." We can say whatever we want to, but what do we do about it? Do our actions show what we care about, what we believe, and what we would sacrifice for?

In the Bible, it often talks of incense being used in the temple. It symbolized their prayers being lifted up to Heaven. I think that is a beautiful description of what is actually happening. In this Psalm, the Psalmist is asking that his prayers be like incense, lifted up to Heaven. His hands are raised with those prayers, not only showing his prayers being lifted up, but also his praise and sacrifice as well. His actions are showing that his faith is in the Lord.

"You see that his faith and his actions were working together, and his faith was made complete by what he did" (James 2:22). We show what we care about by what moves us. We show where our faith lives by where we turn when we need help. We confirm our words by what we do next!

Preparing for Storms

Therefore whoever hears these sayings of Mine,
and does them, I will liken him to a wise man who
built his house on the rock. – Matthew 7:24

Whatever we build, we like to think it's on a firm foundation. Literally speaking, our homes show the importance of this. If something happens to the foundation, the entire home can crumble. This is the same for other parts of our lives – our relationships, our careers, our decisions, and our families – if they aren't built on a firm foundation, they too, can crumble before our eyes.

The end of this passage says, "And the rain descended, the floods came, and the winds blew and beat on that house; and it did not fall, for it was founded on the rock. But everyone who hears these sayings of Mine, and does not do them, will be like a foolish man who built his house on the sand; and the rain descended, the floods came, and the winds blew and beat on the house; and it fell. And great was its fall" (Matthew 7:25-27).

You may not notice your shaky foundation until the storms of life come. A house of cards looks fine until it's shaken. Be prepared by having a strong foundation in Jesus. Then, when these storms come, you will not fall!

May 16

Our Flash Light

Your Word is like a lamp for my feet and a
light for my path. - Psalm 119:105

Whenever you are walking in the dark, using a flashlight, you can only see a few feet in front of you. So, you have to keep that light shining in order to see what is coming next. You can't just shine the light, think, "Okay, I see the way," turn it off, and expect not to bump into things along your way. In the dark, even if you've seen the right path, you can still lose your bearings, veer off course, and fall right on your face!

God's Word is our flashlight in the darkness of this world. We can't just have read it as a little child and then let it sit in our book shelves and think it will do us much good. This light needs to be continually shining in our lives. It may just be a few feet at a time, but it will keep showing us the way. It will keep us from losing our bearings, veering off course, and falling right on our face!

Be Complete in Him

You are complete in Him. – Colossians 2:10

I know that many of you have seen the movie "Jerry McGuire." There is a frequently quoted line from this movie where the main character Jerry McGuire (played by Tom Cruise) says to Dorothy Boyd (played by Renee Zellweger), "You complete me!" Tears flowed from many in the audience when this scene was witnessed.

Many of us seek things of this earth to complete us. Whether it's a spouse, a child, or a career, we seek to find meaning in our lives. Things of this world can disappoint. Things of this world can leave or die or change. If what completes us is of this world, our completeness is always in jeopardy. The Bible tells us "the grass withers and the flowers fall, but the word of our God stands forever" (Isaiah 40:8) and "I am with you always, even to the end of the age" (Matthew 28:20). Make your completeness in Him. Then, and only then, can your completeness actually be complete!

May 18

Super Human Strength

We will find grace to help us when we need it. – Hebrews 4:16

You hear stories of how people can do amazing things when someone they love is in danger. You hear how someone can lift unbelievable amounts of weight, or run into a fire without fear – all to save a child that is in danger. Mothers can hold their sick child without breaking down. Fathers can keep from showing stress when he has lost his job. Parents find the strength to do what needs to be done for their children they love so much.

Can you imagine what our Heavenly Father is able to do for us? If our human parents can do "super human" things for their children, can you imagine what a limitless Father can do? He gives us what we need when we need it. He holds us when we are sick. He comforts us in times of stress. Nothing can keep us trapped if He is our protector. He doesn't need to be forced into super human strength by circumstance, He already has it. He is God! With Him we can face any situation, we can keep our head up, and we can get through!

Believing in Miracles

They came to Him from every direction. – Mark 1:45

During Jesus' earthly ministry, He was constantly surrounded by those who marveled at His teachings and His miracles. They couldn't get enough of Him. Scripture tells us, "and so it was, when Jesus had ended these sayings, that the people were astonished at His teaching" (Matthew 7:28) and that "Wherever He entered, into villages, cities, or the country, they laid the sick in the marketplaces, and begged Him that they might just touch the hem of His garment. And as many as touched Him were made well" (Mark 6:56). Crowds of people believing in Him and receiving His mercy and grace. They believed in His miracles!

My prayer today is that I am always astonished at His teaching. That I am always moved by His mercy and grace. That my trust in Him is as strong as those who risked being trampled just for a chance to touch the hem of His garment. That my faith can move mountains. And that I never stop believing in His miracles!

Hearing the Answer

He answered, "I have told you already and you did not
listen. Why do you want to hear it again?" - John 9:27

Jesus healed a man who had been blind since birth. This formerly
blind man was then interrogated by the Pharisees about who had
done this to him. They asked him, they asked his parents, wanting
to know how this miracle had happened. After asking him again,
he said, "I have told you already and you did not listen." They knew,
but kept hoping for a different answer.

There are times in our lives that we will ask the same questions over
and over again, expecting a different answer. We don't necessarily
like the answer we are getting, so we rephrase or reword trying to
change the answer somehow. Unbelievers will question everything
and anything. They will try any tactic to find a flaw, a loophole, or
an untruth. Don't get discouraged when those you are witnessing
to don't believe. It is our job to share Jesus with others, but the rest
is up to them (and the Holy Spirit)!

May 21

Just Me

Lord, You have searched me and known me. You know
my sitting down and my rising up. – Psalm 139:1-2

Have you been upset about something, but acted like you were just
fine? Have you ever been really excited about something, but acted
like it was no bid deal? Have you ever been around someone that you
don't really like, but acted like you were great friends? Have you ever
just wanted to relax and be yourself, but stopped and thought better
of it? Acting, we've all done it. Why do we tend to hide how we feel,
what we think, and who we really are? Maybe it's fear of not being
accepted, of looking foolish, or of abandonment. There are lots of
reasons why we act rather than just be ourselves.

Jesus knows us. He knows when we are upset, excited, frustrated,
and sad. He knows when we are acting and when we are being
ourselves. He also knows why we do what we do, when we do it.

I love that I can go to Jesus as myself. I don't have to fear acceptance.
I don't have to fear looking foolish. I don't have to fear that He will
leave me. With Him there is no acting, no fear – there is just me!

May 22

No Other Way

Jesus said, "I am the way and the truth and the life. No one comes to the Father except through me". - John 14:6

When I share my salvation testimony with others, I always start with how I acted before I actually got saved. As a child, I guess you can't fully understand what is going on, but I knew I was a sinner. I knew that I wouldn't go to Heaven if I died or Jesus came back before I made a decision. I had come to the "age of accountability" as it is called. But, I wasn't quite ready to make that walk down the isle. So, I came up with a plan. I decided that if I was touching someone who was going to Heaven (or I assumed was going to Heaven), and Jesus returned; then, I would just, by way of attachment, go with them. I know, but give me a break, I was eight years old, this was the best plan I could come up with. The result was that my parents probably thought I was crazy and certainly going to have some major abandonment issues because I wanted to hold their hand all the time! In the end, I decided it was too much trouble and way to risky to try and make sure I was attached to a saved person all the time. So, I finally made my decision, walked down that isle, and gave my heart to Jesus. After that, I realized that life was so much better with Jesus as a part of it. And now, as I grow older, my relationship with Him continues to grow and I can't imagine what I was waiting for.

There are many reasons we can come up with not to give our hearts and lives to Jesus. We can make excuses not to. We can, be like I was, and try to come up with another way. We can also just make the decision not to believe and ignore the outcome. We can wear ourselves out trying to deny the truth. The fact is, there is one way to Heaven and that is Jesus. He's not just the only way, but the best choice for your life. Later, you won't be able to imagine what you were waiting for. Don't look for a way around it, because there isn't one. Ask Jesus into your heart today!

Encourage Each Other

Encourage each other daily, while it is still
called today. - Hebrews 3:13

Have you ever heard the saying, "Don't put off until tomorrow, what you can do today?" This holds true and is beneficial for a lot of things. Encouragement is one of them. I try to remember things that are going on in the lives of my family and my friends. I try to remember to call and say, "I'll be thinking about you today," if something major or stressful is going on. I'll also try to remember to call and say, "How'd it go?" after the fact. I know I really appreciate it when others do that for me, so I try to remember to return the favor. Of course, I sometimes forget, but I do try.

Scripture tells us to, "Carry each other's burdens" (Galatians 6:2). Encouragement is one way to accomplish this. Haven't you ever been really stressed out about something, but a hug or a simple sweet word from a friend, made it a little better? Who do you need to encourage today? Well, get to it!

ஒஇ இஒ

May 24

Needing Peace

Jesus said, "My peace I leave with you; my
peace I give to you." - John 14:27

This word for "peace" or the phrase "peace be with you" is like the
Hebrew word "Shalom". This became a greeting to the disciples
after the Resurrection (John 20:19-26). This peace, God's peace,
is known only to those who believe. It keeps harmony in the heart of
the believer. It calms fears, secures hopes, and suppresses anxieties.
When Jesus said, "My peace I leave with you", He is referring to the
Holy Spirit. A part of Him is left inside the heart of the believer to
help them find their way in this life.

I know that there are times in my life when I have said, "I just
need a little peace." I need to remember that His peace is always
with me. In times of worries, "My peace I give to you," in times
of disappointments, "My peace I give to you," in times when I feel
pulled in all directions at once, "My peace I give to you." No one
understands the need for peace more than Jesus. Let His peace live
in your heart!

ﾉﾚ ﾟﾚﾞ

May 25

Trail Running

Teach me to do your will, for you are my God; may your
good Spirit lead me on level ground. – Psalm 143:10

I have a friend that does "trail running". I had never heard of this
before meeting her. Instead of jogging on pavement or on a treadmill,
which to me is hard enough, she runs trails. When I imagine her
doing this, I think of uneven terrain, with twist and turns, sticks and
rocks underneath her feet, and many obstacles to endure. Sometimes
I wonder, "That's great for exercise, but why does she think that is
fun?" Then, of course, I have to take that thought process to a deeper
level!

Don't we sometimes choose the trails in life instead of the straight
path? Don't we get ourselves into dangerous situations with obstacles
around every corner? Don't we also, at times, think that this is a
good idea or that it sounds like something fun to do? Now, for
exercise purposes, the twists and turns are a good idea, but for your
spiritual life, not so much. The bumps and bruises that come from
this hurt much more. Stop "trail running" in your spiritual life, stick
to the road paved by Jesus!

ೋഇ ഇഔ

May 26

His Loved One

Mary and Martha sent someone to tell Jesus, "Lord,
the one You love is sick". – John 11:3

When I read this verse, I noticed how Mary and Martha didn't say, "Lord, our loved one is sick," but said, "Lord, the one You love is sick." When we pray for others, do we remember that Jesus loves us all? Do we remember that He loves the person we are praying for more than we do?

When someone is sick, when someone dies, when someone gets hurt, many times our friends come to be with us. That makes us feel better. They come give us a hug, tell us that everything will work out, or sit silently and hold our hands. Our earthly friends might not even know this person very well; they are just being our friend. Praying for a loved one is just like that, but better. It's better because you know you are talking to a Friend that loves that person very much!

May 27

One Day at a Time

Do not worry about tomorrow, for tomorrow will worry about its own things. Sufficient for the day is its own trouble. – Matthew 6:34

Abraham Lincoln said, "The best thing about the future is that it comes one day at a time." We spend a lot of time anywhere but in the here and now. We look back at the past, at what we've done, what we've lost, opportunities not taken, and fond memories to ponder. We look toward the future, at what will happen, how we will handle it, the effects our actions will have, and will our loved ones be around. I'm not saying that reflection is bad, it's a good thing to glance back at time, but glance, don't wallow. I'm not saying preparation is bad, we need to plan for our futures, but plan, don't anticipate with worry. Jesus tells us that flowers and birds don't worry, but trust that they will be provided for. He asks that same trust in us!

Maybe this life is given to us "one day at a time" because that's all we can handle. Being in today takes enough of our attention, our energy, and our time. When we spend too much time in our past or in our futures, we might miss a blessing that is only meant for today. Just a moment meant for right now that will never occur again. Trust in Jesus and put your worries in His hands. Face the future with Him walking beside you. And remember, today is important – so don't waste it!

May 28

Accepting One Another

Accept one another, then, just as Christ
accepted you. – Romans 15:7

Are there certain people in your life that get on your nerves? What
is it about them that bothers you? What is it different about them?
Are you harder on these people than you are on others? I have people
like this in my life. I can't always pinpoint exactly what about them
bothers me. Sometimes I can. I also find myself starting to pick on
them for things that don't really matter. Is it because they aren't like
me? Is it because they don't do things like I do? Is it because when
I met them I just happened to be in a bad mood that day? Is any of
this fair to that person?

What if Jesus did this to us? We are not like Him. He is perfect, we
are not. We don't always do things the way He thinks we should.
His way is righteous, our ways are flawed. He doesn't pick us apart.
He loves us and accepts us for who we are. Shouldn't we try to do
the same for others?

Complaining and Arguing

Do everything without complaining and arguing. – Philippians 2:14

Do you know someone who will argue about the color of a sweater? Do you know someone who would complain if their wallet was too small for all of their money? Do you have people that you hesitate to answer when you see their name on caller ID? The hesitation is because you know that you are about to endure at least 15 minutes of complete negativity. Some people seem to make a habit of arguing and complaining and at some point I don't even think they notice it anymore.

Paul said, "I have learned how to be content with whatever I have" (Philippians 4:11). Do you realize Paul was in prison when he wrote those words? He didn't complain, he didn't argue. He spent his time spreading the good news of Christ and encouraging others to do the same.

I know that sometimes I can argue and complain with the best of them, but I don't want to be a person that others don't want to answer when I call. I want to be a person that others are excited to call and share their good news or get encouragement in bad times. I want to be a person that looks at the positive, instead of focusing on the negative. I want to be "content with whatever I have" so much so that complaining and arguing seems silly!

ಅಆ ಆಎ

May 30

Having Abundance

Simon answered, "Master, we've worked hard all
night and haven't caught anything. But because you
say so, I will let down the nets." – Luke 5:5

Einstein said, "The definition of insanity is – trying the same thing over and over again, expecting different results." I can tell you that at some points in my life, this quote holds true. I wore myself out trying to be happy, trying to make things happen, trying to do everything myself. I worked very hard at all the wrong things and nothing ever changed. It's only when I let Jesus in and let Him help that things turned around.

The above passage goes on to tell us, "When they had done so, they caught such a large number of fish that their nets began to break" (Luke 6:6). In other words, Jesus gave them more than they could handle! Wouldn't you like to have such abundance that you couldn't even hold it? Jesus said, "I have come that they may have life, and have it abundantly" (John 10:10). Don't keep trying the same old stuff over and over again thinking that this time it will be different. Come to Jesus and let Him give you an abundant life that's more than you can handle!

･‿ｅ ｅ‿.

May 31

A Simple Man

He had no special beauty or form to make
us notice Him. – Isaiah 53:2

Do we always want to be the center of attention? Jesus didn't. Do we
spend hours getting ready for a party? Jesus didn't. Do we want the
best body, the prettiest face, or the trendiest outfit? Jesus didn't. In
worldly terms, Jesus was less than. He didn't have much in the way
of material possessions, just the clothes on His back. He didn't have
much in the way of status power, just 12 close friends. He didn't have
much, but He had everything!

It's amazing to me how Jesus came. God knew how people would
react if He sent His Son in a blaze of glory, living like royalty. If that
were the case, would their loyalty be genuine? Jesus touched lives
without pretense. Jesus led multitudes without grandeur. Jesus was
just a simple man who changed the world!

June 1

Most Notable Quality

Cain rose up against Abel, his brother, and killed him. - Genesis 4:8

I have a book of different men and women in the Bible*. It gives the "most notable quality" and "most notable accomplishment" of each person listed. For Cain, the most notable quality states "representative of evil" and the most notable accomplishment is "first murderer". For his brother Abel, the first martyr, the reverse is listed. His most notable quality states "representative of good" and the most notable accomplishment is "a heart for God".

In reading this book, I started to wonder what would be listed by my name. What would be my "most notable quality" and my "most notable accomplishment"? Jesus said, "A good man out of the good treasure of his heart brings forth good things, and an evil man out of the evil treasure bring forth evil things" (Matthew 12:35). My prayer today is that when God searches my heart, the good things win out!

*The book mentioned is "10 Minutes to Knowing the Men and Women of the Bible", by Jim George

Whose Are You?

You are Christ's, and Christ is God's. - 1 Corinthians 3:23

I went to a family reunion recently. This was for my grandmother's side of the family, and many of the people that were there I didn't know. While there, when I was introduced to people, they would say, "This is June's daughter", or "This is Liz's granddaughter". Some would even come up to me and say, "Whose are You?" I was known there, by the part of the family I came from or belonged to.

As Christians, we are all a part of the same family of believers (Galatians 6:10). Jesus once said, pointing to his disciples, "Here are my brothers" (Matthew 12:49). Ephesians says, "There is one body and one Spirit, just as you were called to one hope when you were called. One Lord, one faith, one baptism; one God and Father of all, who is over all and through all and in all." (Ephesians 4:4-6).

So, the next time someone asks, "Whose are you?" you know exactly what to say!

๑๕ ๙๑

June 3

The Ability to Forgive

Then he knelt down and cried out with a loud voice,
"Lord, do not charge them with this sin". – Acts 7:60

In this passage in Acts, Stephen was dying. The Jewish leaders were furious by accusations Stephen had made against them. They cast him out and stoned him. Instead of Stephen screaming out for God to avenge his death, or to stop what was happening, or to save his life – he asked that God not hold these people accountable for their actions. This seems so unbelievable sometimes.

Some of us can go for months not talking to someone because they might have hurt our feelings or disagreed with us in some way. We can cut someone out of our lives without blinking an eye. We can't seem to forgive others for things that, in the big scheme of life, don't really matter. When I find myself without the ability of forgive, I need to think of Stephen.

Stephen wasn't concerned with himself or how unfair this was. He was thinking of these people who were hurting him, killing him. He forgave them instantly and asked God to do the same. He had a heart of forgiveness like His Savior's. Jesus said on the cross, "Father, forgive them, for they do not know what they do" (Luke 22:34). Who haven't you forgiven and what are you waiting for?

June 4

Tell Your Story

"Come, see a man who told me everything I ever did". – John 4:29

In this passage of scripture (John 4:1-42), Jesus came upon a women at a well. Jacob's well in Samaria to be precise. Jesus began talking to this woman and telling her of a living water that "whoever drinks the water I give will never thirst. The water I give will become a spring of water welling up to eternal life." Then he proceeded to tell her things about herself that a stranger could have never known. Instead of being embarrassed or ashamed, she felt joy. Instead of being angry or defensive, she ran to share her story with others. She heard him and believed.

When we realize that Jesus knows everything about us, it should bring us joy. It shouldn't bring embarrassment or shame because we've been found out. It shouldn't just bring relief that you don't have to tell Him. I hate the feeling I get when I have to admit a wrong to someone. My stomach hurts and I lose sleep. I don't have that anxiety with Jesus. I just have to go to Him and say, "I'm sorry." And all He says is, "I forgive you, now it's done." No lecture. No guilt trip. No "look at what you've done!" Just love and grace and mercy and forgiveness! Like this woman at the well, we should run and tell our story!

◌◌◌

June 5

Silly Superstitions

Guard what was committed to your trust, avoiding the
profane and idle babblings and contradictions of what
is falsely called knowledge – by professing it some have
strayed concerning the faith. – 1 Timothy 6:20-21

I was thinking today about superstitions. Superstitions, psychic networks, daily horoscopes, even fortune cookies – when taken seriously, can be dangerous. Sounds silly doesn't it? Silly until a Friday the 13th comes around and you automatically think it's going to be a bad day. Silly until a black cat runs across the street in front of your car. I used to have a friend that would turn around and go the other way!

Scripture tells us to "avoid the profane and idle babblings and contradictions of what is falsely called knowledge". The world is full of advice from so called "help" in finding our way. We, as Christians, have to be careful were our advice and "help" comes from. It's a confusing world out there, so don't be fooled by silly superstitions. Don't get me wrong, I'm still going to eat my fortune cookie, I'm just not going to bank on what's inside. Stay in God's Word. Keep those daily prayers and quiet times coming. Praise God that with him in your life, everyday is a good day – even Friday the 13th!

Forgiving the Undeserving

Having confidence in your obedience, I write to you, knowing
that you will do even more than I say. - Philemon 21

I will admit, I had never read the book Philemon until this morning.
This is a letter, from Paul, to Philemon. Philemon was supposed noble
man, who was the owner of a slave, named Onesimus. Onesimus
apparently had stolen from Philemon and then ran away. Paul is
requesting that Philemon, having probably become a Christian
during Paul's ministry in Ephesus, forgive Onesimus, who had also
become a Christian while Paul was in prison, for whatever wrongs
he had committed.

After reading this letter, even though it never states what Philemon
decided, it shows that Paul had complete confidence that he would
forgive Onesimus and continue to serve the Lord along side of this
former slave, turned friend.

Even in situations were the forgiveness might not be deserved, as
Christians we are to follow Christ's example. Letting go of the
past and moving on, helps all involved. Holding on to bitterness
and angry is counter productive. Philemon could have followed the
law and had Onesimus killed for his crimes or out of love he could
have forgiven his brother in Christ, which do you think he chooses?
Which would you choose?

ᵒᵍᵉ ᵍᵉᵒ

June 7

God of the Impossible

Abraham fell facedown; he laughed and said to himself, "Will
a son be born to a man a hundred years old? Will Sarah
bear a child at the age of ninety?" – Genesis 17:17

The Bible is full of stories of the impossible. One I always remember is Isaac being promised to Abraham and Sarah. Both past the age of usual parenthood, they thought the idea was a little comical. Sarah even took matters into her own hand and gave Haggar to Abraham and Ishmael was born. If she could have only remembered that with God, nothing is impossible. And true to His Word, God gave them Isaac. This promised and long awaited son came into their lives.

We ask God to give us the impossible all the time. Why then, do we tend to not believe that He will actually do it? We grow weary of waiting sometimes and take matters into our own hands. Usually, not bringing desired results! Wait on God's time. Trust that He will give you what you need. Don't laugh at the impossible. Know that with God, nothing is impossible!

I Am Willing

And behold, a leper came and worshipped Him, saying, "Lord,
if you are willing, You can make me clean." Then Jesus put out
His hand and touched him, saying, "I am willing; be cleansed."
Immediately his leprosy was cleansed. – Matthew 8:2-3

"I am willing." Those beautiful words that came from Jesus' mouth
are spoken to all of us. Here He is helping a man with leprosy, a
very visible disease. Everyone knew what was wrong with this man.
What about those problems that we don't let anyone see? Is He
willing then?

He is willing! Willing to calm your storm. Willing to give courage to
your fears. Willing to erase your doubt. Willing to give you anything
you might need. He is willing to help, are you willing to let Him?

June 9

Turn on the Light

Everything exposed by the light is made clear. – Ephesians 5:13

Do you often walk around in the dark? Even if it's familiar territory like your home, I bet you don't keep it pitch black when you are up moving around. Why? Is it because you might have left some shoes in the middle of the floor that you might trip over? Is it because you might get up in the night still a little groggy and bump into the furniture? Is it because you are afraid that some crazy person might be waiting behind the door to jump out and grab you? (That last one is for me!)

When you want to be sure where you are going, turn on the light. When you want to make sure nothing will make you stumble, turn on the light. When you are afraid of what might jump out and grab you, turn on the light. Jesus said, "I am the light of the world. He who follows Me shall not walk in darkness, but have the light of life" (John 8:12). When you want to see everything clearly, turn on the Light!

June 10

Learn to Be Content

I know what it is to be in need, and I know what it is to
have plenty. I have learned the secret of being content
in any and every situation, whether well fed or hungry,
whether living in plenty or in want. - Philippians 4:12

I think about this verse a lot. I quote, "learn to be content in any situation" to myself quite often. This life is full of ups and downs, twist and turns, the unexpected and the predictable. If I could be like Paul, and "learn to be content in any situation," I would never have stress again.

Paul's saying that he's been rich and he's been poor, and he was just fine either way. He loved the Lord Jesus and wanted to serve him, and that's exactly what he did. Everything else in life was just filler in between. When he was on his mission trips, he was content with life. When he was in prison, he was content with his life. And in the end he said, "I have fought the good fight, I have finished the race, I have kept the faith" (2 Timothy 4:7). Notice he didn't say, "And I whistled and skipped all the way!" He knew this life was a race, a fight, and sometimes a struggle, he accepted it because he believed in what he was fighting for...... and that made him content!

Life is not always going to go our way. We aren't always going to feel like dancing. Just remember in the race we are running, believe in what we are fighting for and learn to be content!

᧧᧪᧧

June 11

Ordering by Sight

For man looks at the outward appearance, but the
Lord looks at the heart. – 1 Samuel 16:7

Once, when I was on a cruise with my family, at dinner every night we would get dessert (I know, not a good idea!). Three nights out of the five, I got this chocolate cake that was wonderful. My mother, who never once ordered this cake, would tell everyone that was thinking of ordering it that it was too rich. I asked her, "How can you say that when you have never eaten it?" She replied, "Well, I can just tell by looking." Well, she was wrong, that cake was wonderful!

Many non-believers do this same thing to Christians. They might say, "That church is full of hypocrites," even though they have never been through the doors. They might assume, "All those Christians are self-righteous and judgmental," possibly not knowing any of them personally. And even though they have no proof to their accusations, they will tell this same thing to their friends.

When people look at you, what will they see? Will they see that self-righteous, judgmental, hypocrite they assume you are? Or will you prove them wrong by having the beautiful characteristics of Jesus? Do you show love or hate? Do you show peace or struggle? Do you show caring or indifference? Would they want to order what they've seen in you or will they send you back to the kitchen?

Saving Faith

If people say they have faith, but do nothing,
their faith is worth nothing. - James 2:14

We can say we want to lose 10 pounds, but if we don't watch what we eat or start exercising is it something we truly want? If we say we want to work on a certain relationship, say with a spouse, family member, or friend, but don't start communicating, isn't that like saying "Actually, I don't care that much"? We've all been there. We make wishes or goals, but really never put out the effort it takes to obtain them.

In the above verse, James isn't saying that this someone actually has faith; he says that they just claim to have it. He is describing someone who shows no external proof of the faith they so often claim.

Our actions usually show where our passions lie, where our priorities are, and what motivates us. Just like I can believe that I truly want to lose 10 pounds when I find myself at the gym, I can believe in the saving faith that I claim, when it shows in what I do!

June 13

Spilling Over

My cup overflows. - Psalm 23:5

Have you ever really pictured what this verse is saying? I know that at times, when I have been making myself something to drink, I accidentally let it get too full, making the liquid come up over the sides. The drink then comes over the top, spills down the sides, then proceeds to the counter - and even on those lucky occasions, it makes its way down to the floor!

Think about this when counting your blessings. We are so prone to see what we don't have, we forget to stop and think about what we do. I'm positive that if you sat down and started counting your blessings, they would come up over the top, spill down the sides, get all over the counter, and proceed to flood the floor! Don't be a part of this negative thinking world. As the old hymn says, "Count your many blessings, name them one by one. Count your blessings, see what God has done!"

One Key

Ask, and it will be given to you; seek and you will find;
knock, and it will be opened to you. – Matthew 7:7

Have you ever walked to your door, at night, and had trouble finding
the right key to get in your door? Maybe you didn't leave the porch
light on. Maybe you didn't get the right key ready before leaving
your car. Maybe there are so many keys on your key ring that
finding the right one can be difficult. As you fumble in the dark,
your frustration builds because you know there is only one key that
will unlock that door and allow you to go inside.

When we are fumbling in the darkness of this world, looking for a
way into the light inside, Jesus is the One (the only) Key that will
work. He is the One Key to salvation and to life. Jesus said, "I am
the way, the truth, and the life. No one comes to the Father except
through Me" (John 14:6). There are many keys on the key ring of
life. Don't keep trying the wrong ones; use the One that gets you
through the door!

June 15

The Twinkling of an Eye

We shall all be changed - in a moment, in the twinkling of an eye, at the last trumpet. - 1 Corinthians 15:51-52

The word twinkling means rapid movement. Also, the eye moves faster than any other part of our external bodies. Most of the time, you don't see that it has moved or changed its view. So when we say that life can change in the twinkling of an eye, that doesn't leave time to act. So, instead of waiting to act, when there won't be time to act, we need to prepare.

Just in case of a car crash, we wear our seat belts. In order to not fall down stairs, we hold on to the guard rails. In preparing to jump out of an airplane, we first put on a parachute. We try to be ready for all possible "in the twinkling of an eye" seconds.

Scripture tells us that "every knee will bow, and every tongue will confess to God. So then, each of us will give an account of himself to God" (Romans 14:11-12). We will all someday know that Jesus Christ is Lord. We will all someday look into His face. This will happen in the twinkling of an eye. Don't go into this "in the twinkling of an eye" second unprepared, believe in Him today!

June 16

Be Still

Be still, and know that I am God. - Psalm 46:10

I was having a conversation with a friend about how hard it is to make a decision, an important, life-altering decision, when you have no clue what to do. Sometimes, I can pray and pray about something and still not know what to do. That's when I always recite this verse to myself, "be still, and know that I am God" (Psalm 46:10). Because if I don't, I tend to make mistakes due to rash actions on my part. I get tired of waiting for something to happen or an answer to be clear, so I take matters into my own hands, do something or say something impulsively, and regret it almost instantly.

Waiting for God's plan to play out in your life can be a frustrating battle if you cannot remember to "be still, and know that He is God". Remember that He wants what's best for you, "I have come that you might have life, and have it abundantly" (John 10:10). And His plans are far better than anything we might come up with, "No eye has seen, no ear has heard, no mind has conceived what God has prepared for those who love him" (1 Corinthians 2:9).

Patience has never been a really popular and accomplished virtue. Take some time today, to step out of your stress, let go of your questions for a minute, stop waiting on edge for an answer, and just "be still"!

June 17

Life is a Battlefield

The One who is in you is greater than the one
who is in the world. – 1 John 4:4

Your life is a battle. A spiritual battle. Satan (the one who is in the world) is constantly trying to trip you up, make you fail, and ruin your witness and your life. This is a fact we should all accept. Your Christian life isn't easy, it's a battlefield!

Did you notice in this passage that it does not say "you" are greater, but it says "The One who is in you" is greater? This means without Jesus, you will not defeat Satan. You will lose. So, tip the scales in your direction by having Jesus on you side. Be prepared by studying His word and praying daily. Surround yourself with faithful soldiers instead of double agents. This way, when the saints go marching in, you will be with them!

June 18

Wheat and Roses

Let both grow together until the harvest, and at the time
of harvest I will say to the reapers, "First gather together
the tares and bind them in bundles to burn them, but
gather the wheat into my barn". – Matthew 13:30

When I was little, I can remember my grandmother having a beautiful rose garden. She would go out to her garden, with her shears, and cut some of the roses. As she was doing this, she would also prune the bushes – cutting off the thorns and dead leaves and throwing them into a pile. She would also pull weeds from the ground and add them to this pile to be discarded later. In the end, the discarded pile would be burned (because back then you could still burn things in your yard) and the roses had found a place in her home, displayed in all their beauty.

Jesus is coming again. He will come out to the harvest of man to separate us into "tares and wheat", "weeds and roses." Chose Him. Believe in Him. Put your faith and trust in Him. Don't be cast off with the tares and the weeds, have your place in His home, displayed in all His beauty!

Tell Him About It

Give all your worries to Him, because He
cares about you. - 1 Peter 5:7

A lot of times, we don't share our worries and stresses with others because we don't want to bother them. We can sometimes have this same attitude toward God. We can convince ourselves that He has bigger and more important things to attend to, and doesn't need to be interrupted by our issues. We tend to forget that God created the world in seven days; I assume He's a pretty good at multi-tasking!

The truth is that He cares about everything that has to do with you. The Bible tells us that "even the very hairs on your head are all numbered" (Matthew 10:30). If He cares about something as small as how many hairs you have on your head, I think He cares about what's keeping you up at night! Tell Him about it today!

The Timeless Word

The entirety of Your Word is truth, and every one of Your righteous judgments endures forever. – Psalm 119:160

I know someone who told me that he thinks the Bible is a great book of history, but is now outdated. He thinks that the world has changed too much for the Bible to still apply. Sadly, I think there are more and more people thinking this way. Suddenly, using Bible principles for your life makes you old fashioned and behind the times.

The Bible tells us "to love one another" (John 13:34), to "not worry about tomorrow" (Matthew 6:34), to not be judgmental and to forgive (Luke 6:37). It teaches us to have mercy and compassion (Luke 6:36). There are many, many other wonderful and timeless principles that teach us how to live our lives. If more people had the capacity to love others, to not spend so much time worrying about things they cannot control, to be able to forgive others and even themselves, to show compassion to the lost and suffering – how wonderful would this world be?

꧁ ꧂

June 21

Our Behavior

Be an example to all believers in what you say, in the way you
live, in your love, your faith, and your purity. – Timothy 4:12

When I started working with the youth at church, one of them asked
me, "How do I witness to kids at school?" I told her that I think the
best witness we can have is our behavior. How we act and how we
react to the circumstances around us is the first witness others will
see in us. It will speak louder than anything we could possibly say.

We can know the answers to the tough Biblical questions. We can
have a testimony ready to tell anyone who might ask. We can even
have a heart to bring others to the Lord. But, if we don't show in
our behavior that we are a Christian, who is going to know to ask
us those hard questions, or want to hear our testimony, or to know
that we are about them in the first place? How is your behavior and
will it attract others to seek what you have?

There's Always Cause
to Rejoice

How shall we sing the Lord's song in a foreign land? - Psalm 137:4

Most of the time, our lives are pretty routine. We go to work, we take care of our kids, we run errands, wash clothes, etc. When anything unexpected messes with our routines, we can feel like we are in "foreign" territory. One of the meanings of foreign is "alien in character" - meaning, it's not normally what you do. When our lives are out of normality or character, do we always feel like praising Jesus?

Scripture tells us to "rejoice always" (1 Thessalonians 5:16). That is sometimes really hard to do, but read on, you can really tell that divine inspiration was at work here. It's a lot easier to "rejoice always", when you combine this with "praying continually, and giving thanks in all circumstances" (1 Thessalonians 5:17-18). It's hard not to praise Him, when you first seek His comfort in prayer and top it off by counting your blessings. When I do that, it doesn't really matter what else is going on, there is always cause to rejoice!

ᴐⱺᴊⱺᴐ

June 23

Undivided

Give me an undivided heart. – Psalm 86:11

I will never forget something that was said during the sermon the day my Godson, Cole, was Christened. The pastor said, "Life can't have a divided focus". I have thought about and prayed about that phrase many times since hearing it.

Some people "ride the fence" spiritually. They know right from wrong, profess to be a Christian, but show no evidence of it. I use to be one of these people. I thought I could live in both worlds, have a divided focus, "ride the fence"; but now I know that is impossible. I didn't ever live in both worlds! I only pretended to live in one and did live in the other. "No one can serve two masters" (Matthew 6:24). I could not have ever had a true relationship with God while living a sinful life. Now, I try to live my life focused on what God wants me to do and how He wants me to live. Am I saying that now I am perfect? Far from it! What I am saying is that now I am trying.

It is my prayer daily that my life never has a divided focus, to no longer "ride the fence", and for my actions to show that I serve only one master, Jesus!

≈⊛ ⊛≈

June 24

His Strength

My grace is sufficient for you, for my power is made
perfect in weakness. - 2 Corinthians 12:9

I don't know about any of you, but sometimes I feel like the harder
I try to do what is right, the harder Satan works to show me that I
can't. If I try to be more patient, then he throws circumstances at
me where patience feels impossible. If I try to be more humble and
selfless, then he plays on my insecurities. If I try to be more giving
and compassionate toward others, then he places people in my path
that I find it hard to feel sorry for. Like I've said before, Satan's been
playing this game for a long time, and he knows what he's doing.

When I've gotten to the point where I have reached a limit within
myself, I try to remember, "My grace is sufficient for you, for my
power is made perfect in weakness". If I can remember this, then
I can think of my weakness as a gift because that is when His
strength steps in. Only then can I be a little more patient, can I be
a little more humble and selfless, can I be a little more giving and
compassionate - even if I don't really feel like it!

June 25

He Loves You

For God so loved the world that He gave His only son, that whoever believes in Him shall not perish, but have everlasting life. - John 3:16

The only thing you ever have to remember is that God loves you. He loved you before you were born, and He has loved you everyday since. Right or wrong, good day or bad day, whole or broken, God loves you. There isn't a whole lot in this world that is for sure, but this is!

God loves us, and all He asks is that we believe that - that we believe in Him. Hold on to His love on a bad day, rejoice in His love on a good day, and have peace in His love in all those times in between!

⸙⸙⸙

June 26

There's Always Hope

As Jesus passed on from there, He saw a man named
Matthew sitting at the tax office. And He said to him, "Follow
Me." So he arose and followed Him. - Matthew 9:9

Matthew was a tax collector, making him outcast in Jewish society.
His profession was filled with corruption and despised by many.
But, as Jesus passed Matthew, He saw something in him that no
one else could see. He saw obedience, faith, and goodness. So when
Jesus said, "Follow Me". Matthew left everything behind and never
looked back.

Matthew is a reminder for all of us not to judge a book by its cover.
There are many out there that we might see as "beyond hope". Well,
there is always hope in Jesus. Jesus loves the unlovable. He forgives
the unforgivable. He finds worth in the unworthy. I'm certainly glad,
because He did all of this for me!

ഔളള

June 27

Have Faith in Storms

Jesus was in the stern, asleep on the cushion. - Mark 4:38

In this passage of scripture, Jesus and His disciples were crossing a lake. As soon as they ventured out, a fierce storm started raging. During all the chaos, Jesus was asleep. The disciples were screaming for help and woke Him up. He stood up, and silenced the storm with a word. Then, He turned to them and asked, "Why are you afraid? Do you still have no faith?" (Mark 4:40).

Even though it can seem, at times, that Jesus is asleep in the midst of our storms, be assured, He is not. He is always there with us, even if, at the time, He seems silent. He knows when the time is right to step in and calm the storm. There are going to be storms in this life and He will get us through them. So, the next time you're screaming out for help, remember His words, "Why are you afraid? Do you still have no faith?"

Broken Thinkers

Trust in the Lord with all your heart, and do not rely
on your own understanding. - Proverbs 3:5

Once, a counselor was talking to a group of alcoholics and addicts
in the rehabilitation facility where she worked. One of her newer
patients, wanting to defend her actions, started talking and began
with, "Well, I think", and this counselor quickly interrupted and
said, "Stop right there. That's your first mistake. Stop thinking. Your
thinker is broken. Because your best thinking got you here!"

Sometimes, when we rely on our own understanding, this life doesn't
always make sense. When we rely on our own thinking, we can end
up in a real mess. We need to depend on Him for understanding
and pray for guidance in our thinking. If we do, our thinkers won't
be broken and one day, we will see Him in heaven and He will smile
and say, "See, your best thinking got you here!"

๑๑ ๑๑

June 29

He Has No Limitations

I will never leave you or forsake you. – Hebrews 13:5

I sometimes put human limitations on God. I think that He might not come through for me, because most of the people in my life at least once, have failed me. I am also pretty sure that there have been times when I have failed them. Don't get me wrong, I'm not blaming here, I'm just stating that human love and human relationships are flawed. They are flawed because we, as humans, are flawed. We cannot be perfect, so therefore, our actions and emotions and relationships cannot be perfect either.

I feel ridiculous when I realize that I have put human limitations on God. He is perfect! His love is perfect! His timing is perfect! He will never leave me or forget me or not care what happens to me. He has a love for me that I will never be able to comprehend. He has a plan for me that I could never have dreamed for myself. He is always there for me and has no limitations!

All I Need

The Lord is my shepherd, I shall not want. – Psalm 23:1

In some translations, this verse ends with "I have all I need." Have we ever actually thought that what we have is enough? Don't we always want more? When I was little and I would tell me mother that I needed something, she would say, "Do you need it, or do you want it?" I, of course, always answered that question with "I need it!"

Jesus gave us everything we need through His death and resurrection. He is all we need. He will provide all we need. He gives us salvation, strength, comfort, guidance, and many, many other things. When we learn to distinguish the difference between an eternal need and an earthly want, we will finally say, "I have all I need, because I have Jesus!"

July 1

The Freedom of Forgiveness

*They sinned against me, but I will wash
away that sin. - Jeremiah 33:8*

Do you know who Jesus forgives? Everyone who asks. I sometimes wonder if there were a few in the crowd that day who cried, "Crucify Him!", who later came to Him with sorrow for what they had done. I wonder if a few of those soldiers who cast lots for His clothes realized that He was who He said He was. I wonder if the one who drove the nails in His hands wished that he could take that moment back. The amazing thing is - if they did ask for forgiveness, Jesus gave it to them!

No matter what we have done in our lives, Jesus forgives. He forgives and He forgets. He showers us with His mercy, His grace, and His love forever. Come to Him today and see what the freedom of forgiveness feels like!

༺ ༻

July 2

Just a Few

Who will hear about all these decrees and say, "Surely this great nation is a wise and understanding people?" - Deuteronomy 4:6

Obedience to God's law not only made the Israelite nation stand out both morally and spiritually, but that obedience was also a witness. It was not just something that benefited them individually, bringing them closer to God, but also had a chance to bring others to the Him as well. When they were successful in their obedience, they were feared among nations and they were blessed. Rahab, the harlot, said of what God had done for His people, "When we heard of it, our hearts melted and everyone's courage failed because of you, for the Lord your God is God in Heaven above and on the earth below." (Joshua 2:11). She risked her life and the life of her family for a God she had not known before. Why? Because of what she had seen and heard He could do.

We can, as a nation, show how blessed a nation can be who follows the Lord. You know how that starts? With you and with me. It wasn't the whole Israelite nation that came into Rahab's home; it was two men seeking shelter from harm. It wasn't the whole Israelite nation that showed mercy for her and her family, it was two followers of the One True God. It doesn't start with as one nation under God; it starts with just a few! Let's start with a few and grow from there. Let's show all other nations how blessed we can be!

July 3

It's Hard to Be Humble

Blessed are the meek, for they shall inherit the earth. - Matthew 5:5

What does being meek mean? Growing up I tended to think that meek meant wimpy, but that is not true. Meek means humble. Humility is an admirable, but rare character trait these days. Can you think of someone who you think of as a humble person? I can and I probably have more respect for that person than any other person I know.

Scripture tells us that, "God opposes the proud, but gives grace to the humble" (James 4:6). There are many things that are so important in God's Word that we, in our human nature, find it so difficult to do. Love, forgiveness, and humility are three that come to mind first. Can we love with an unconditional love? Can we forgive and let it go? Can we be humble in a world that sees this as weak? The old song says, "Oh, Lord it's hard to be humble." I think this song writer is right. That may be why those who are "shall inherit the earth!"

July 4

God Bless America

If my people, who are called by my name, will humble
themselves and pray and seek my face and turn from their
wicked ways, then I will hear from heaven and will forgive
their sin and will heal their land. – 2 Chronicles 7:14

Our pastor preached on this verse one Sunday, typical around this
time of year. His message was entitled, "Where is God in America?"
It got me thinking about those great nations throughout history that
aren't around anymore. I thought of Babylon, Rome, and as recent
as the former Soviet Union. These were great and feared empires,
but where are they now?

America is a great nation, but we need to be careful not to forget
Who made us great. This nation was founded as "One Nation
Under God". Where is God now? We need to humble ourselves and
remember how we got here. We need to be thankful for the blessing
of being born here. We need to pray that God will continue to bless
America!

ഀൟ ൠ഍

July 5

He's Everything

"I am the Alpha and the Omega," says the Lord God, "who is, and
who was, and who is to come, the Almighty." – Revelation 1:8

I was in a Bible study and we were discussing the constant presence
of God. We don't worship someone who did some good things, had
some wise deep thoughts, and then died. We worship a living God,
an eternal King, and a constant Promise. He was here before time,
He is here in the present, and He holds the future.

John said, "In the beginning was the Word, and the Word was
with God, and the Word was God" (John 1:1). When Moses asked,
"Whom should I tell them sent me?" God said to him, "I am Who I
am. Tell them, I Am has sent you" (Exodus 3:13-14). "I AM" – that's
present tense, that's constant, and that's always!

Our God is not a memory of a good person who made a dent in the
history of our world. He is so much bigger than that! He is alive and
He is here with us. He is the Alpha and the Omega (for those who
don't know, these are the first and last letters of the Greek alphabet).
That's like us saying, "He's from A to Z!" He's everything!

186 | *Leigh Ann Madding*

July 6

Go in Peace

Jesus said to the woman, "Your faith has
saved you; go in peace." – Luke 7:50

We try many things in this world to get some peace. We get messages, take bubble baths, do yoga, and take vacations – all in order to get some peace. There is a whole division to the pharmaceutical industry whose purpose is to calm down the stressed and anxious. We again and again seek to find what only Jesus can truly give.

There is a reason that one of the names of Jesus is Prince of Peace. He can give you the peace that your heart needs. He can give you the joy that doesn't depend on the things of this world. He can give you the love that never fails. He is the one who can say, "Your faith has saved you; go in peace!"

༺ℭ ℭ༻

July 7

God is With Us

But Moses protested to God, "Who am I to appear before
Pharaoh? Who am I to lead the people of Israel out of Egypt?"
God answered, "I will be with you." – Exodus 3:11-12

When God called Moses to bring the Israelites out of their bondage
in Egypt, Moses didn't feel like he was the best candidate for the
job. He pressed this point to God saying, "What if they don't believe
me, and then what do I say? What if they ask me who you are?"
God answered, "I am Who I Am." (Exodus 3:13-14). Moses said, "I
am not very good with words. I never have been." God said, "Who
makes a person's mouth? I will instruct you in what to say" (Exodus
4:10-11). Moses said, "Send anyone else!" The Lord said, "All right,
take your brother Aaron with you. I will be with you both" (Exodus
4:13-15).

Moses didn't have faith in himself, but God did. Moses didn't have
a clue what he would accomplish in his life, but God did. God knew
that through Moses, He would do a mighty work. Why? Because
God knew that He would be with Moses – every step of the way!

In the different ministries of Christ, we may feel like we can't do
this or do that, but God can. We may feel we aren't the right fit for
something, but God is. We might feel that we will fail, but God
won't. As long as we remember that God said, "I will be with you",
we can accomplish things we could have never imagined for Him.

Stop Falling

If you do not stand firm in your faith, then
you will not stand at all. - Isaiah 7:9

There have been times in my life when my faith was so flimsy, that I was always finding myself face down in the dirt. I would go along, face an obstacle, and a lot of times, I would trip and fall. I was under the impression that I just had bad luck. It wasn't bad luck, it was lack of faith. I didn't pray before I made my decisions. I didn't think, "What would Jesus do?" I didn't trust in anyone but myself. I wasn't running the race of life; I was fumbling my way through.

Faith in Christ is the foundation of our lives. Without this firm foundation of faith, we don't stand a chance at stability. I'll admit to still getting shaky sometimes, but I do not continually have to pick myself up out of the dirt anymore. I heard once that, "If you don't stand for something, you'll fall for anything." How true that is! Stop falling, stand with Jesus!

꧁꧂

July 9

No Shadows Here

Every generous act and every perfect gift is from above,
coming down from the Father of lights; with Him there is
no variation or shadow cast by turning. - James 1:17

I have heard this verse many times, although usually just the first part. The "every perfect gift is from above" part is really big at baby showers! But, I've never really paid attention to the end of this verse before. When it says "Father of lights," this was an ancient Jewish expression for God as the Creator. The reference to "lights" means celestial bodies (sun, moon, stars), which all change from day to night, all rotate, all cast shadows. In short, they don't stay the same.

As Revelation says, "I am the Alpha and the Omega," says the Lord God, "Who is, and Who was, and Who is to come, the Almighty" (Revelation 1:8). In a world were everything is always changing, and everything has a shadow, I'm so thankful that God doesn't. "Every generous act" comes from an unchanging God that always loves and always has compassion. "Every perfect gift" comes from an unchanging God that always knows what's best. Our God is never in the shadows, but always in the light!

July 10

Strong Witnesses

Don't set foot on the path of the wicked; don't proceed
in the way of evil ones. - Proverbs 4:14

When I was younger, I thought I could be around certain things, go
to certain places, and be around certain people because I was strong
enough to resist the temptations I might be faced with. Jesus dined
with sinners too, right? I also thought I could date guys that might
be a little questionable because I could be a good influence. I could
help them find their way. Salmon married Rahab, the harlot, didn't
he? I knew just enough of the Bible to be a danger to myself. Just
enough to try and justify my actions.

The truth is I need to remember that I'm not as strong as Jesus. I
can't dine with sinners and not be influenced by their actions. I
can't go into dangerous situations thinking, "Well, I'll just be a
witness to them." And those questionable guys, I seem to forget that
Rahab changed before Salmon married her, not after. We all have
different weaknesses. We all have different strengths. I could go to
a casino and never be tempted to spend all my money. I might not
have that same luck at a bar.

Be a strong witness in those situations that don't tempt you. Stay away
from those that do. That's why God made us all unique; we can be
strong witnesses in different situations and in different ways!

July 11

Precious in His Sight

When you pass through the waters, I will be with you; and
when you pass through the rivers, they will not sweep
over you. When you walk through the fire, you will not be
burned, the flames will not set you ablaze. - Isaiah 43:2

I have to tell you, this is one of my favorite verses in the Bible. Its
beautiful description of security always makes me feel better just by
reading it. There are times in life when you don't think you can take
one more thing. There are times when you don't feel the strength to
carry on. And there are times when you think, this is it, I'm done.
Those are the times, when I remember these words. This is God
saying, "No matter the circumstances, I'm here and everything is
going to be alright!"

This passage goes on to tell you why everything is going to work out,
it says, "Because you are mine, and precious in my sight!" In a world
where we sometimes feel that we don't matter, we matter to Him. In
a world that's too busy with its own problems to worry about yours,
you are His concern. In a world that can seem to not care, He does.
Why? Because you are His, and you are precious in His sight!

This Day

This is the day the Lord has made; let us rejoice
and be glad in it. - Psalm 118:24

There was a guy at work and every morning he would say, "Today is going to be a great day isn't it?" One those mornings when my coffee hadn't quite kicked in yet, I found myself thinking, "What's wrong with this guy? He must be medicated. No one is that happy in the morning." Then one day, after passing him in the hallway, and him singing his usual happy tune, I sat down and read this verse. I was the one that had something wrong, I just needed a reminder. Thank you Lord for teaching me this lesson!

We can choose whether or not to face our days assuming they will be bad or we can think, "Today is going to be a great day!" As Christians, everyday is a good day because we have Jesus in our lives. There will be ups and downs along the way, and some days will be more difficult than others, but He is with us every step of the way. This is the day that the Lord has made, I will rejoice and be glad in it!

≈૭૨ ૭૨≈

July 13

The Lost Coin

Rejoice with me, I have found my lost coin. - Luke 15:9

Have you ever known you had a $20 bill somewhere, but you couldn't remember where you put it? You've looked in your wallet, checked your pockets, cleaned out your purse, and even looked in the car - still nothing? How happy and relieved were you when you finally come across it?

The Parable of the Lost Coin shows how even one coin is valuable and special. This woman had 9 more, but searched and searched for the one that was lost. When she had found it, she looked to her friends and said, "Rejoice with me, I have found my lost coin!"

The meaning of the parable is simple. Everyone is valuable to Jesus! He may have saved thousands upon thousands by His love and His grace, but He is still concerned about those who are still lost. We should care too! Who are the lost coins in your life? Help find them be found today!

July 14

Fight for God's People

If I must die, I must die. – Esther 4:16

In the story of Esther, she saved the Jews from a massacre. Like so many before, the Jews had an enemy, and his name was Haman. He was plotting to kill all the Jews he could. Esther, being in the presence of the king, begged for their salvation, knowing that revealing herself as a Jew could cost her life. She answered her call with, "If I must die, I must die."

We still have an enemy, Satan. He has always been here and he always will. We, like Esther, have to fight for God's people. We have to put ourselves out there, spread the Word, and help others come to know Jesus. We have to spread the Word for the salvation of the lost. Jesus commanded us to, "Go therefore, and make disciples of all the nations, baptizing them in the name of the Father and of the son and of the Holy Spirit" (Matthew 28:19). In this time, and in this country, it will probably not cost us our lives, but just a little of our time, just a little of our money, and just a little of our unselfishness. When I think of Esther, what I'm asked to do isn't much!

July 15

Trail of Bread Crumbs

This is what the Lord says: "Stand at the crossroads and look;
ask for the ancient paths, ask where the good way is, and walk
in it, and you will find rest for your souls." - Jeremiah 6:16

In reading this verse, I thought of the children's story, Hansel and Gretel. As disturbed as I am as an adult, finally realizing that this story was about a carnivorous grandmother-like character, waiting in the woods to eat children; it did have one part that applies here - the trail of bread crumbs. The children, not wanting to lose their way, left a trail of bread crumbs to help show them the right path home. Unfortunately, the trail they left was scavenged by the animals of the forest and they got lost and fell into danger.

We have all wandered. Some more than others, but we all lose our way sometimes. We need to have a way back home. But, the way needs to be paved with things that "moth and rust do not destroy, and where thieves do not break in and steal" (Matthew 6:20). As I'm writing this, the verse, "Give us this day our daily bread" (Matthew 6:11) comes to mind. Asking God to give you "daily bread" is an excellent trail of bread crumbs that can't be taken away and will always help you find your way back home!

ౣఄఴ

July 16

What's Next

> But one thing I do: Forgetting what is behind and
> straining toward what is ahead. - Philippians 3:13

Looking back. So many of us do it. How many stories are written, songs are sung, and poems are quoted about looking back? How many dollars are spent on therapy for those haunted by their past? The what was and the what ifs that come into our thoughts. Memories aren't meant to be traps, they aren't meant to shut us off from life. We are only to learn from our past, grow from it, enjoy remembering the good things, and let go of those things that we cannot change. As I write this I am reminded of the "Serenity Prayer" - "God, grant me the serenity to accept the things I cannot change, the courage to change the things I can, and the wisdom to know the difference." Popular prayer, often quoted, yet so hard to do!

If you are walking through life looking back, you can't see where you are going. Eventually, you will trip and fall over something you can't see. Take the advice of Paul, "forget what's behind and strain toward what's ahead." Look to the One that helped Paul do this, Jesus. Once, when I was wallowing in self-pity about something from my past, a dear friend looked at me with her sweet smile and asked, "Why can't you just accept God's grace and move on?" Simple question, with an obvious answer. Christ can help you get past, and move forward to a life spent with Him. A life full of His love, His mercy, and His grace! A life where you will excitedly say, "What's next?"

࿐ ౿ ౿

July 17

Problem Child

Even children are known by the way they act, whether their conduct is pure, and whether it is right. - Proverbs 20:11

Everyone who has worked in the church nursery always has a certain child in mind that they secretly hope might not be there the Sunday they have to work. Sounds harsh, I know, but it's still true. There might be a child who disrupts the other children, doesn't mind, is extremely loud, or is a bully to the other kids, who knows - we have had them all!

Another thing to notice is when the parents come to pick up this problem child. The look on their face tells it all. It's almost like their eyes are pleading, 'Please tell me he/she has been good. Just this once?" They don't have to see what their child has done to know. They know their own child that well!

God knows us even more then our own parents do. He knows us even more than our friends, our spouse, or our children. He sees how we act in every situation. He sees how we respond to those around us. He sees "whether our conduct is pure, and whether it is right." If you could see the face of God, what would He look like when He comes to pick you up? Would His eyes be saying, "I know My child has behaved badly and I'm sorry you had to deal with him/her" or would He say, "I told you he/she was a joy. I might be a little prejudiced, but was I not right?" Don't be a problem child, be the child everyone wants to keep!

July 18

Forever Thirsty

Everyone who drinks this water will be thirsty again, but whoever
drinks the water I give him will never thirst. - John 4:13-14

I don't know about you, but this verse means a lot to me. If, like
me, you have tried other means to gain comfort, acceptance, relief,
love, peace, etc; you know that any means other than Jesus doesn't
last. Anything this world provides as a substitute is temporary, but
Jesus is eternal.

Whether you turn to alcohol, money, drugs, sex, shopping, work,
self-help books, or anything else, these things cannot keep you full.
You will constantly be going back for more. These things can't love
you back and you will still feel alone. These things don't care what
happens to you, they are not affected. These things confuse the
truth, because only Jesus is the truth. Turning to Jesus fills you and
keeps you full. Coming to Him when you are in need, keeps you
comforted and feeling safe. Who or what do you turn to instead of
Him? Are you quenched or will you be forever thirsty?

July 19

Are You Listening?

Speak, Lord. I am your servant and I am listening. - 1 Samuel 3:9

In this passage of scripture, Samuel is hearing from the Lord for the first time. He didn't know what it was the first few times, and then finally he said, "Speak, your servant is listening." He didn't know what God was going to say. He didn't know what God was going to ask. He did let God know he was willing because he said "your servant". If a master tells a servant to do something, does he get to say, "Well, I don't think I want to do that?" Not in those days! When Samuel said, "I am your servant", he meant, "Tell me what you want me to do and I will do it!"

We are better at talking to God than listening to Him. Don't get me wrong, we are supposed to go to Him with our hopes, our needs, and our fears. I guess my point is, when was the last time you listened for Him? When was the last time you asked what He wanted from you? In other words, when was the last time you said, "Speak, Lord. I am your servant and I am listening?"

The Faith of Abraham

Then he brought Abraham outside and said, "Look now toward Heaven, and count the stars if you are able to number them." And He said to him, "So shall your descendants be." - Genesis 15:5

Abraham was an old man and childless when God made him this promise. I have often prayed for the faith of Abraham. He didn't question. He just obeyed and trusted. He had complete faith in God's promises. Two verses came to mind while writing this. "No eye has seen, no ear has heard, no mind has conceived what God has prepared for those who love Him" (1 Corinthians 2:9), and "And we know that in all things God works for the good of those who love Him, who have been called according to His purpose" (Romans 8:28).

Believe in the promises of God. Trust in His love and in His time, and you will have life, and have it abundantly (John 10:10). Pray with me for the faith of Abraham. He had the faith to believe that even an old man could become a father of an entire nation. Why? Because God said he would!

Firm Foundation

He is like a man building a house, who dug down deep and laid the foundation on rock. When a flood came, the torrent struck that house but could not shake it, because it was well built. - Luke 6:48

In looking at your relationship with Jesus, how firm is your foundation? We are going to have difficult times. We are going to be tempted. We are going to need something inside ourselves that is stronger than we are alone.

When the storm comes, lean on Jesus. When temptation comes, put Him in front of you. When you need faith and hope, talk to Jesus. Include Him in whatever is going on in your life. When you lay your relationship with Jesus on a firm foundation, you will come out on the other side of any difficulty still standing!

Heaven on Earth

Your kingdom come. Your will be done, on
earth as it is in Heaven. - Luke 11:2

Have you ever heard someone say, "This is Heaven on earth!"? I
sometimes say that when eating something with lots of chocolate!
We all play around with phrases about Heaven and wonder what
Heaven will be like. One thing we do know is that, in Heaven, an
eternity is spent praising God.

We are to praise God. We are to praise Him in times of joy and
peace. We are to praise Him in times of sorrow and strife. David
said, "I will bless the Lord at all times; His praise shall continually
be in my mouth" (Psalm 34:1). Praising God is part of His will for
us. Scripture tells us to "Rejoice always, pray without ceasing, in
everything give thanks; for this is the will of God in Christ Jesus
for you" (1 Thessalonians 5:16-18). In doing these things, I think we
come as we can get to Heaven on earth!

ᴏᴏᴇ ᴇᴏᴏ

July 23

Lot in Life

Lot chose the entire Jordan valley for himself. - Genesis 13:11

In the Old Testament story of Lot, the nephew of Abraham, he and his uncle divided their land, each taking a piece for their families and their herds. Abraham let Lot chose which part of the land that he wanted for himself. He chose the most promising looking land and left the rest for his uncle. This promising looking land was in the region of Sodom and Gamorrah. Time pasted and Lot, who already had wealth, prospered even more, only to lose it all when God destroyed these wicked cities.

Greed can overtake many in their journey to find fulfillment. When you make decisions about money, jobs, opportunity, and even moving from one place to another, seek God's guidance. Pray. Trust in Him. When He tells you to go, go. And when He tells you to get out, don't wonder, "What about all my stuff?" The Bible tells us, "Do not store up for yourselves treasures on earth, where moth and rust destroy, and where thieves break in and steal" (Matthew 6:19). Don't make money more important than God. Don't make your earthly possessions more important than Heavenly rewards. Learn from this story and just ask yourself, "What's the Lot in your life?"

ഗ്ഗ ഗ്ര

July 24

No Comparisons Necessary

A person is made right with God not by following the law,
but by trusting in Jesus Christ. - Galatians 2:16

We need to beware of self-righteousness. I'll admit, I've have had
my moments with this character defect, and compare myself with
this person or that person. But the trick is, I instantly pick someone
that, I think, gives me the advantage. In these moments, I'm
quickly reminded why self-righteousness isn't a good look on me
and I usually get around to finding my flaws anyway, so this strategy
doesn't really work. No matter how I compare myself to this person
or that, God's grace is not something I could ever earn or deserve, no
matter how much I justify it. What I (and all) need to realize is that
no matter how good or how bad a person is, we all need Jesus!

I thank Jesus everyday for being the best part of me. The only part
worth anything. I know that nothing I do has meaning anything
unless He's a part of it. I know that my life isn't worth anything
unless His will is guiding it. No comparisons necessary. Just me! I
have not been made right by anything I've done or not done, I've
been made right through the love and grace Jesus!

No Juggling Act

I have not lost any of the ones that you gave me. - John 18:9

I did not receive the gift of hand-eye coordination. I could never dribble a basketball between my legs. I couldn't twirl a baton very well. Having said that, I'm always amazed when I see someone juggling. Especially, when they have more that two to three balls in the air. I'm usually just waiting to see what trips them up or which ball falls to the ground first. When that happens, when just one ball drops, it all seems to fall apart.

Even though we can sometimes feel like a ball being juggled in the air, we won't get dropped. When our lives feel like we are going in circles, Jesus can help us to stop and have peace. When we give our hearts and lives to Him, we will be included when He says, "I have not lost any of the ones that you gave me." His is no juggling act, one where we are waiting to see what trips Him up and who falls to the ground. He holds on to us no matter what!

꧁꧂

July 26

No More Take Backs

You have heard that it was said, "You shall love your neighbor and hate your enemy." But I say to you, love your enemies, bless those who curse you, do good to those who hate you, and pray for those who spitefully use you and persecute you. – Matthew 5:42-44

How easy is it to be nice to someone who has been nice to you? Pretty easy. How easy is it to be nice to someone who has done something to hurt you or irritate you or slander you? Not very easy! For a silly example, just think about when you have road rage. These acts by other drivers are often unintentional, but we still seem to have a fit about it and say and do things that are not very nice!

We will always have those in our lives that make things difficult, that hurt us, or make us sad. There are going to be those that could care less about anyone but themselves. These acts can be both intentional and unintentional. But, we don't have to let their actions turn us into bitter, angry people. Jesus tells us that if someone slaps you on your right cheek, turn the other to him also (Matthew 5:39). If we focus on getting back, holding grudges, temper tantrums, bitterness, and resentments, we are hurt more than the person these feelings are about.

I have grown in the knowledge that Jesus doesn't tell me to act this way because He wants to give me a difficult "to do" list for my life. It's because it's the right thing to do. It's because His way brings the best outcome. His way brings no guilt about something I might have done in anger. His way doesn't leave me wishing I had a "take back" for a hasty reaction. His way doesn't leave me growing in anger and bitterness, but instead growing in the peace and joy that comes with living in Him!

July 27

Remembrance of Me

Do this in remembrance of me. - Luke 22:19

Today, July 27, is a reminder for me. On this day, years ago, I said goodbye to an old life and started over with a new one. But, you can't ever leave every thing behind. Your memory still remains. I used to think of this as a handicap, but now, I see it as a blessing. On this day, I can remember what I'm capable of when I don't keep God close. On this day, I can remember what His love, forgiveness, grace and mercy can do. And on this day, I can remember that I have no right not to show this same treatment to others.

I have been told "I hope you can just forget and move on." My prayer is that I don't. The above verse, taken from the first Lord's Supper, comes to my mind on this morning. My prayer is that every time I've been forgiven, "Do this in remembrance of me;" every time His grace and mercy has known no bounds, "Do this in remembrance of me;" and every time His love takes my breathe away, "Do this in remembrance of me!" What He has done for me, I hope I never forget to give it to those around me!

July 28

Are You a Peacemaker?

*Blessed are the peacemakers, for they will be
called children of God. - Matthew 5:9*

Do you remember when you were in high school and a fight would
break out? Soon the two fighting would have a crowd around them
watching. Some in the crowd would even be cheering for one kid or
the other. Finally, a teacher would have to push their way through
the cheering crowd to break up the fight.

Are you a peacemaker? If you hear a juicy piece of gossip, can you
keep it to yourself or immediately call to tell someone? If one person
is angry with another, do you fan the fire or try to put out the flame?
If someone has hurt you, do you seek revenge or do you turn the
other cheek? It is not always easy to be a peacemaker or to do the
right thing. Remember, God blesses the peacemaker, for they will
be called children of God!

Praying for the World

Lord, teach us to pray. - Luke 11:1

Jesus is a wonderful teacher. I receive His lessons daily if I'm paying attention. Sometimes, these lessons come in the form of a humbling experience. The minute I think, I'm pretty good at this; He smiles and says, "My precious child, you still don't have a clue!" I was in a meeting once, and the speaker said, "What if, for the past year, all of your prayers had been answered, the way you wanted them to be answered, then how different would the world be? Or, would it just be your world that was different?" Wow, again, I realized, I have a lot to learn on how to pray.

I never forget to pray for my needs, for my concerns, for my hopes and for my dreams. I usually don't forget to pray for my family, my friends, and those things around me. I have to be reminded sometimes to pray for my country, for those I don't know who are lost, and for those around the world who need Him as much as those in my small speck of space. No matter how much I think I've grown, there's always room for more. I need to wake up every day and say, "Lord, teach me to pray!"

༺ུ⁙༻

July 30

Unexpected Peace

*I have told you these things, so that in me
you may have peace. - John 16:33a*

There are moments in life when I need some peace, His peace. It can be when work is busy, when my mind can't stop racing, or when people disappoint. Jesus finds a way to give me peace. Peace first fills my heart, then that spreads to my mind. I sometimes fight against it with my ignorant human will, but when I let go, He fills me from head to toe with contentment and peace. He has an unlimited supply and I love when it comes in the most unexpected moments.

There are times when I can be in the midst of a crying fit and He comes in and soon I'm smiling. I can be in the midst of a temper tantrum and He comes in and settles me down. I can be in the midst of plotting some sort of mischievous revenge and He comes in and makes it seem silly. I can be feeling overwhelmed with life and all that comes with it and He reminds me, "In this world you will have trouble. But take heart! I have overcome the world" (John 16:33b). If your heart is open, peace will come - even in those moments when you least expect it!

July 31

You Can Be Free

For he had often been chained hand and foot, but he
tore the chains apart and broke the irons on his feet. No
one was strong enough to subdue him. – Mark 5:4

This man in scripture, which is also talked about in Matthew 8 and
Luke 8, was tormented by demon possession. No one could help
him and no one could restrain him. He ended up living alone in
caves and other solitary places. Jesus came and freed this man from
his tortured life.

Do you have something in your life that tortures you? Something
you have tried to rid yourself of? Something you have tried to "chain
down" or restrain? There is one solution to your problem and that is
Jesus. He is not only willing, but He is able. He can succeed where
all human efforts have failed. Trust in Him today and place in His
capable hands what is torturing you. It is by Him and through Him,
that you can be free!

August 1

Time to Pray

O God, You are my God; early will I seek You. - Psalm 63:1

I don't know about any of you, but I talk to my mother every morning. I get to work, get settled, and then give her a call. I don't always have something specific to say, in fact, most of the time I don't. This is just our routine. Some days, if I get really busy or have an early morning meeting, I don't call. Later, when I do find time to call her, she always says, "Well, I was wondering. I'm just use to hearing from you by now." That is partly because my mother is a worrier, but it's also because not talking breaks our normal routine.

Seeking time to spend with God needs to be a part of our daily routine. We don't have to have something specific to say. We don't have to wait until tragedy strikes or when we have a request that needs His attention. Wouldn't it be great if our prayer time was so frequent that if we get busy and don't pray, God Says, "Well, I was wondering. I'm just used to hearing from you by now!'?

August 2

My People

I will live with them and walk with them. And I will be their
God, and they will be my people. - 2 Corinthians 6:16

Do you have a certain person that you share everything with? I do. I
call them "my person." Actually, I have a few, "my people", I guess.
When something is going on, and I can't reach one of them and talk
things through, it's like I don't know what to do. When I stop and
think of who "my people" are, I wonder, where is God on this list?

Jesus wants to be a part of our lives. He wants us to share everything
with Him. He wants to be the One we run to and guess what? He's
never unreachable. Scripture tells us, "I will live with them and walk
with them. And I will be their God, and they will be my people." I
know I'm considered one of "His people," what I need to make sure
of is that He's included as one of mine!

August 3

What Do Others See?

Your cleansed and obedient life, not your words, will bear witness to what I have done. - Luke 5:15 (The Message Bible)

In this passage from Luke 5, Jesus had healed a man who suffered from leprosy. After doing so, Jesus told him not to go around town telling what had happened to him, but only to show himself - cleansed.

Don't tell others, show them. I think that is a wonderful plan for those who have been changed by God's grace. Those around us will believe what they see much more than what they hear. I can tell others all day long that I am a Christian and that God's grace is amazing, but what they need to see is proof in my actions. They need to see that I am different. My prayer today is that when others look at me, they see compassion in my eyes, truth in my witness, and love in my heart. I pray that they see Jesus in me!

August 4

My House

As for me and my house, we will serve the Lord. - Joshua 24:15

The above verse is seen displayed in many homes. It might be on a plaque or in a picture placed in a place for all to see. I've always passed right by it thinking, it's just me at home. I always assumed this verse was for those with a house full of people, a family. Today when I saw it, I thought of something different. Even though it's just me, I'm still there. I don't have to have a house full of people to have a house that serves the Lord.

What I do when I am home, what I watch on TV, the music I listen to, the websites I look at, the books I read, all make up how I spend my time and in part make up who I am. I need to be aware that everything I do matters. Everything I do, whether at home alone or when I am with others, influence the values I have and the decisions I make. So, I need to remember these words, "As for me and my house, I will serve the Lord!"

August 5

Your Light

Then God said, "Let there be light." - Genesis 1:3

We have all had a storm come through during the night and we wake up to no electricity the next morning. It is extremely difficult to get dressed and ready for work when you can't see. Things are always easier when you have some light!

When storms come through our lives, our light can get wiped out. It is hard to get prepared for what comes next when you can't see. Jesus said, "I am the light of the world. He who follows Me shall not walk in darkness, but have the light of life" (John 8:12). Even when you don't know what's coming, Jesus does. Keep Him, your Light, close to you. With Him, your light is never wiped out, you are never unprepared, and you are always ready for your day - whatever it may bring!

August 6

Daily Nourishment

Give us this day our daily bread. - Matthew 6:11

When I am going through something difficult, I tend to eat too much. I have a friend that is the opposite. When she goes through hard times, she loses a ton of weight (I know, I hate her too!). Even though we are at opposite ends of the spectrum, we both have the same problem. We have no clue what we need. What is too much and what is not enough?

This passage from the Lord's Prayer (Matthew 6:9-13), states "give us this day our daily bread." We ask that He give us, daily, the spiritual nourishment that we need. Jesus knows when we need a little and when we need a lot. He knows when He needs to walk along side of us and when He needs to carry us. He knows when we are weak; He is strong!

We need spiritual nourishment in a "one day at a time" manner because, "Therefore do not worry about tomorrow, for tomorrow will worry about its own things. Sufficient for the day is its own trouble" (Matthew 6:34). Ask Jesus to give you what you need today and tomorrow, ask again!

August 7

Radiance and Glory

And we, who with unveiled faces all reflect the Lord's glory, are being transformed into His likeness with ever increasing glory, which comes from the Lord, who is the Spirit. - 2 Corinthians 3:18

In Exodus 34, Moses was speaking with God. He wasn't aware that, when he faced the Israelites after that his face had become so radiant they were afraid to come near him. Following this time, when he would leave the presence of the Lord, he would put a veil over his face before speaking to the people. Because of their fear, he would hide from their view, the glory of God. To this day, that same veil "covers their minds so they cannot understand the truth" (2 Corinthians 3:14).

There are many today with a veil over their hearts. Some sort of barrier that keeps them from understanding the truth and seeing the glory of God. Something in the way that is blurring their view. But, "whenever anyone turns to the Lord, the veil is taken away" (2 Corinthians 3:16). When that veil is taken away, the glory of God shines through those who believe in Him. Shed your veil today and let the radiance and the glory of God shine through you!

August 8

Be Moldable

But the pot he was shaping from the clay was marred
in his hands; so the potter formed it into another pot,
shaping it as seemed best to him. - Jeremiah 18:4

My daily prayers include that I be in God's will, that I be the person He wants me to be. In order to do this I have to be flexible and moldable. I may not get to do everything my way or how I think things should be done. I have to conform to the image of Christ and sometimes that is not comfortable.

When I don't feel compassion, I have to be molded into a person who cares. When I am angry, I have to be molded into a person who forgives. When I am stubborn, I have to be molded into a person who submits. I have to let Him do the shaping and molding of my life and my character. If not, I know that trouble awaits!

August 9

The Good Shepherd

*"I am the good shepherd; and I know my sheep,
and am known by My own." - John 10:14*

In this passage in John, Jesus calls Himself, "The Good Shepherd."
He talks about how the shepherd goes before the sheep and they will
only follow his voice (John 10:4). The sheep will scatter when they
hear the voice of a stranger (John 10:5). He warns that a hired hand
will run when danger approaches and leave the sheep behind (John
10:13). He promises to lay down his life for his sheep (John 10:15).
He came so that we could have life (John 10:10).

As Christians, we are His sheep. Our Shepherd cares what happens
to us. He will guard us when danger approaches. He will come and
find us when we stray. He did not save Himself, but laid down His
life for us. Jesus is the Good Shepherd and He does know His sheep!
He knows what we need, what dangers we face, what is going to
happen next, and He wants to help!

August 10

Sleep Well

Do not let the sun go down on your wrath. - Ephesians 4:26

Whenever I read this verse, I think about those times that I was so mad about something that I couldn't sleep. Even if I do manage a short nap, it wakes me up and I start thinking about it again. Maybe there is a reason for that? Maybe I'm not supposed to sleep until the anger is resolved.

Anger is a powerful emotion. It changes, hurts, and damages people. There is a healthy anger - ex. being angry about child abuse or world hunger - but that doesn't seem to be the anger that festers in the soul. The anger that comes from unforgiveness comes first to my mind. Being angry with someone else, someone you can't bring yourself to forgive hurts your more than the person you are angry with. Let it go! Most of the time, nothing can be done to change what you're angry about, so just try to move past it. If you can do this, I feel certain that inner peace will come! (At least it did in my life.) Don't let the sun go down on your wrath, and sleep well!

Live with His Joy

*These things have I spoken unto you, that my joy might remain
in you, and that your joy might be full. – John 15:11*

I have had several conversations with people about the difference
between happiness and joy. There are those in this world that seem
to be under the impression that God's going for their lives is that
they are supposed to be happy. Not true! There is not reference in the
Bible that promises that we will be happy. It tells us that we will be
persecuted for His name's sake. It gives us a promise of His peace and
joy when we ask for it. It tells us of His love, compassion, mercy and
grace. It offers salvation to anyone who wants to accept it. Wonderful
stuff in the Bible, but nothing that promises happiness.

God has a bigger purpose than our happiness. What about your
obedience? Obedience isn't always easy and won't always bring giddy
happiness. What about your compassion? If you have never been sad,
how can you know compassion? What about standing up for Him?
If you have never had a disagreement about your faith, do people
really know you have one?

You can have God's joy without being happy. I can have a really bad
day and still stop and smile when I think of Him. I can be upset and
disappointed in this world, but still feel His comforting arms around
me. I don't have to be happy. God's joy is enough for me. Do I want
to be happy? Of course, but I have realized that it is not what's most
important. The world is bigger that what's happening in my life.

August 12

If You're Happy and You Know It

Happy are the people whose God is the Lord! - Psalm 144:15

Once, when on vacation with my family, my nephew, who was eight-months old at the time, was with us. Every morning, we would read his favorite book that had been adapted from the children's song, "If You're Happy and You Know it." His face would just light up when he saw that book. My 5 year old niece liked not only to read it, but to act it out for him.

This simple message from a children's book teaches something that should be true in our lives. We have a loving God who has saved us from death. We have a compassionate God who is there for us when we need Him. We have a merciful God who picks us up when we fall and forgives us when we mess up. We should be the happiest people on earth! I'm not asking you to "clap your hands" or "stomp your feet," but if you're happy and you know it, then at least let your face show it!

August 13

Put Down Your Anchor

This hope we have as an anchor of the soul,
both sure and steadfast. - Hebrews 6:9

When you are on a boat and you want to rest and stay where you are for awhile, you put down the anchor. This helps the boat stay in place when the water is rough or when the wind blows. It even helps when the water is calm, because the boat just naturally veers off into a direction that you might not want to go. In these cases, the boat could float into water where, under the surface, there are dangers that you cannot see.

Jesus is the anchor in the boat of life. He keeps us steady and calms the storm. He gets us through the rough water. He can see the dangers that are unseen to us. Ask Jesus into your life, put down your anchor, and rest in Him.

August 14

A Lesson from Legion

And he cried out with a loud voice and said, "What have I
to do with You, Jesus, Son of the Most High God? I implore
You by God that You do not torment me." - Mark 5:7

In this passage of scripture, Jesus came upon a man who was being possessed by many demons. So many, when Jesus asked this demon's name, it (they) said "Legion", meaning "for we are many." What amazes me most about this passage is that the demons knew exactly who Jesus was. They said, "What have I to do with You, Jesus, Son of the Most High God?" They knew who He was and they also knew His power and that is why they begged that He not torment them. They didn't question Him, they just knew.

From His birth, there were many who didn't believe Jesus was the Son of God. No matter what He said and no matter what miracles they saw Him do, they denied His name, His power and His purpose. I read this passage and think, "even demons believed in Jesus." Why is it so hard for so many to believe in Him? And for those of us who do believe in Him, why don't we believe in what He can do? I hate to say, learn a lesson from Legion, but at least they didn't doubt!

Back on Track

Though You have made me see troubles, many and
bitter, You will restore my life again; from the depths of
the earth You will again bring me up. - Psalm 71:20

Many times after a hectic day, a crisis is seen through, and a seemingly endless state of confusion finally clears; Jesus is there. He gives life renewal of strength and substance. He sets the record straight on what's really important, sets us back on our paths, and holds our hands along the way.

In the midst of your difficult time, remember, "Though You have made me see troubles, many and bitter, You will restore my life again, from the depths of the earth You will again bring me up!" What an awesome reminder that through Him, no matter what we are going through, we can always get back on track!

August 16

His Discipline

Endure hardship as discipline; God is treating
you as sons. - Hebrews 12:7

We have all seen parents who will submit to a screaming child. The child will pitch a fit until the parent finally caves and gives the child what they want. This might seem the path of least resistance at the time, but in the end, it doesn't teach the child anything. Because later in life, no matter how much you scream, you don't always get what you want. Why? Because you don't always need what you want. God, as our Heavenly Father, teaches us to trust Him, and one way is through discipline. In short, His saying, "No, you can't have that. You don't need it."

The above scripture goes on to say, "No discipline seems pleasant at the time, but painful. Later on, however, it produces a harvest of righteousness and peace for those who have been trained by it" (Hebrews 12:11). When God tells us no, He's not just being mean or difficult. He is letting us know that we need to wait, or trust, or just know that we don't always know what's in our best interest. That's what a parent does. Trust in His discipline and don't pitch a screaming fit, it won't work with Him!

Being With God

Then Moses said to Him, "If your Presence does not go
with us, do not send us up from here." - Exodus 33:15

Moses had led God's people out of their bondage in Egypt. He
was leading them to the Promised Land, "into a good and spacious
land, a land flowing with milk and honey" (Exodus 3:8). They were
trading a life of slavery to a life of freedom. Moses, instead of just
being glad to be out of there, was concerned about continuing to be
in the presence of God. He was saying, "If You don't go, I don't want
to go either." It didn't matter to him how perfect this Promised Land
was, if God wasn't going there with them, he wanted no part of it.

Moses wanted to be with God and to be set apart by God. He also
wanted others to know that God was with him, that God was on his
side, and that all he had was because of God's awesome power and
wonderful mercy. The Lord said to Moses, "I will do the very thing
you have asked, because I am pleased with you and I know you by
name" (Exodus 33:17).

Moses didn't live to see the Promised Land, but gained everything he
wanted because he only wanted to be in the presence of God. He is
remembered as being a great man of God, who believed, trusted, and
obeyed. He left a life of privilege to be an outcast. He fought against
the powers of this world with the power of God. He led God's people
through the wilderness beyond the temptation and the strife that
journey brought. He did none of this on his own, and he knew it.
Through it all, God was with him. Why? I believe there are many
reasons why, but one stands out today - because he asked!

August 18

What He's Capable Of

Not only so, but we also rejoice in our sufferings, because we
know that suffering produces perseverance; perseverance,
character; and character, hope. - Romans 5:3-4

I don't always cherish the bad moments in my life. Who does? But, I do cherish those moments in which Jesus brought me out of them, shows me that He's always there, and that no matter what happens, I'm going to be alright because I am His. If I never need His grace, how would I ever know that it is sufficient (2 Corinthians 12:9)? If I am never weak, how would I know His strength (Psalm 73:26)? If I was never ignorant, how would I know His wisdom (James 1:5)? If I never need Him, how would I know what He's capable of (1 Corinthians 2:9)?

I always hurt for those who haven't experienced the impact of what Jesus can do in a life. I long for them to get a glimpse inside my heart and witness the brokenness He has mended, the darkness He has shone a light through, and the incompleteness that He has made whole. I wouldn't wish my sufferings on anyone. I wouldn't recommend the bad choices I've made in life. But, I will never stop thanking Jesus for getting me through, picking me up, and loving me no matter what! We all have suffering. We all have bad days. We all make bad choices. Why don't you let Him show you what He's capable of?

༄༅ ༅༄

August 19

Being Teachable

Jesus said to her, "Mary." She turned toward Him and cried out
in Aramaic, "Rabboni!" (which means Teacher). - John 20:16

I have heard the story of the resurrection many times. In reading this
passage this morning, I noticed what Mary called Him, "teacher."
In her excitement at seeing Him, this was the first word she said.
Jesus is called teacher many times in scripture. In fact, while He was
living on earth, He's called teacher as much or more than anything
else. The definition of teacher is "someone whose occupation is to
instruct." Think about that for a minute.

As Christians, it is essential that we be teachable. If I'm paying
attention, Jesus teaches me lessons daily. Why do teachers teach us
lessons? So, when we are tested, we will pass!

Life brings all sorts of tests and trials along the way. Being teachable
is one way to prepare you for whatever might come. Being teachable
shows that you are willing to listen and learn from Jesus and His
Word. Being teachable shows the humility that brings His strength.
Being teachable helps you pass the test of life!

August 20

What Gets You Fired Up?

Peace I leave with you, My peace I give to you; not as
the world gives do I give to you. Let not your heart be
troubled, neither let it be afraid. – John 14:27

I have to confess something to you. I sometimes fight the urge to
be really ugly. When I moved into my home, I was going back and
forth with the cable company for weeks with no results. I was so
mad one afternoon that I actually called a few friends to pray for
me. I kept repeating "Be kind to one another" (Ephesians 4:32) in
my head. Okay, so I sometimes have a temper. One morning during
this ordeal, I read "A gentle answer turns away wrath, but a harsh
word stirs up anger" (Proverbs 15:1). I smiled and said, "Okay Jesus,
I know!"

What struck me like a ton of bricks was a voice in my head saying,
"Why don't you get this fired up over Me?" Ouch! I stared wondering
why I got so worked up about my DVR not working, but don't feel
the same frustration about the lost world around me. Why I got
upset that I might miss one of my favorite shows, but don't always
pay attention to a friend that has missed a lot of church lately? My
prayer today is that I don't let the little stuff get so important that I
forget about the big stuff, His stuff! I don't know if you suffer from
the same problem, but you are welcome to pray this with me!

August 21

Building Faith

Human life comes from human parents, but spiritual
life comes from the Spirit. – John 3:6

As we were growing up, most parents tried to give us everything
we need. They gave us food and shelter. They gave us support and
love. They gave us guidance and discipline. There is one thing your
parents cannot give you, your faith. They can give you a belief
system. They can start the process, but they cannot build your faith.
You have to do that on your own.

As an adult, I realized that my parents had given me a wonderful
foundation in Christ. I also realized that I had to build a faith of
my own. I wasn't going to fight temptation using my father's faith. I
wasn't going to grow in Christ using my mother's faith. I needed to
build a faith of my own. Not just a belief, but a faith. Start building
on your foundation of faith today!

ͼʡ ʡͽ

August 22

A True Friend

Since they could not get him to Jesus because of the crowd, they made an opening in the roof above Jesus and, after digging through it, lowered the mat the paralyzed man was lying on. - Mark 2:4

In this story in scripture, a paralyzed man had some determined friends. They fought the crowd, and still saw no way to get their friend to Jesus. They climbed up onto the roof and still saw no way. They didn't give up! They tore through the roof, and lowered their friend into His presence. Through their determined effort, their faith in Jesus, and their love for their friend, this man was saved!

What would you do to get your friends to Jesus? We need to fight the crowd. We need to climb a mountain if we need to. We need to tear through the barriers that are in our way. Whatever it takes to get them into the presence of Jesus!

We need to be an example for our friends who are watching. We need to pray for our friends who are struggling. We need to show them the light, so that they can find their way. Don't give up! We need to be a friend like this man in scripture had, a true friend!

August 23

Only One Way

I am the way, the truth, and the life. No one comes
to the Father except through Me. -John 14:6

There are many "so-called" faiths today that gives followers many
different roads to Heaven. According to them, being good can get
you there. Good works and effort can get you there. Self-will can get
you there. There are even some that say there is no Heaven or hell.
A few of these faiths have even started as Christians faiths that have
now been perverted in some way. We are warned in scripture to not
be fooled by false doctrines. Paul writes to Timothy, "Now the Holy
Spirit tells us clearly that in the last times some will turn away from
the true faith; they will follow deceptive spirits and teachings that
come from demons" (1 Timothy 4:1).

There is a Heaven. There is a hell. There is only One God. There is
only one way to Him and that is Jesus Christ. Anything else you are
told or that you read is just not true! Don't assume you know what
the Bible says, read it for yourself. The Bible clearly tells us that some
will turn away from their faith. Don't be one of those people!

August 24

Be Usable

Pursue peace with all people, and holiness, without which no one will see the Lord: looking carefully lest anyone fall short of the grace of God; lest any root of bitterness springing up cause trouble, and by this many become defiled. - Hebrews 12:14-15

Once, our pastor preached a sermon on this passage. It was about the bitterness that is spawned by unforgiveness. So many people suffer from it. I say "suffer" intentionally. Because those I know that have bitterness from unforgiveness do suffer. Sometimes, if this bitterness isn't dealt with, they can suffer their whole lives. The sad part is, some of these suffering people, are Christians.

He focused part of the sermon on the word "defiled." Defiled means contaminated or stained. He went on to talk about a shirt he had with an ink stain on it. The shirt is not really useful anymore, but because it was a gift from His son, he won't get rid of it. It will just be put in the back of his closet and it will just stay there. Almost like he hopes that somehow the stain will go away and he can wear this shirt again.

The point is, bitterness defiles us and makes us unusable. We can be so consumed that we can't do anything else. But, since we are God's child, we can even look at it like we are a gift from His Son, He won't get rid of us. John 10:29 says, "no one is able to snatch them out of My Father's hand", and this means Satan and his use of bitterness. But, because of our weakness for it, we might be set aside and left to sit in the back of the closet until Jesus returns. This isn't God's will for our lives. We are to "pursue peace with all people, and holiness, without which no one will see the Lord!" Don't be a bitter person that misses out! Let the love and grace of Jesus wash your stain away! Be usable to the Lord!

August 25

Help My Doubt

But I trust in Your unfailing love; my heart
rejoices in your salvation. – Psalm 13:5

Once, a man knocked on my door. I answered because he had a small child with him (smart man!). He wanted to talk to me about Jesus. I told him that although I was blessed to see his efforts, I already knew Jesus as my Savior and he should go on to someone who didn't already trust in the Lord. For some strange reason, I thought of this yesterday. After the memory replayed in my head, I heard that "still, small voice" saying, "Do you really trust Me?" Of course, my immediate answer was "Yes, Lord. You know I trust You." Then, the scripture that I have come to understand so much, "I do believe; help my unbelief" (Mark 9:24) came to the surface of my mind.

If I trust so much in Him, then why do I worry about the future or things that are out of my control? If I trust so much in Him, then why do I still try to do things my way instead of His? If I trust so much in Him, then why do I sometimes whine about the unfairness of life? Trusting in Jesus isn't just something you claim, it's something you do. I'll admit that it's not always easy. It takes prayer. It takes studying His Word. It takes discipline. It brings belief and faith together. It also takes His help. In times of wavering say, "I do trust You, Jesus, but please, help my doubt."

ஒ௦ ௦ஒ

August 26

The Essential Part

God is at work within you, helping you want to obey Him, and
then helping you do what He wants. - Philippians 2:13

I'm often amazed at those who say that they need to get their life straightened out before they get involved in church or start working on a relationship with God. Really? That's like saying, "I really need to lose some weight before I start dieting or go to the gym."

You need God's help to obey Him. You need His guidance to let you know what He wants from you. This happens through spending time with Him in prayer, in His Word, and in times of praise and worship. So many things of the spiritual nature are not of human nature. Don't wait until you feel ready or you never will be - you will always be missing the essential part. You can't "get your life straightened out" without Him!

August 27

Staying Silent

Watch your tongue and keep your mouth shut, and
you will stay out of trouble - Proverbs 21:23

How many of you have said, "Oh, I wish I hadn't said that?" I have many times. For me, it is when I feel threatened, scared, or angry, that my "not-so-good " side comes out. In those times, I say things I don't mean and in the worst cases, things I can never take back.

Sometimes, what we say can get us into more trouble than what we do. In these times, we would do better to abide by the golden rule, "Do unto others as you would have them do unto you," or in this case "talk to others as you would have them talk to you." We know what words can hurt. We know how we want others to talk to us. Why then can't we either do that or just stay silent? Did your mother ever tell you, "If you can't say something nice, just don't say anything?" I think that was "divinely" sent advice!

August 28

Up or Down?

Carry each other's burdens, and in this way you
will fulfill the law of Christ. - Galatians 6:2

In regard to others' spiritual growth, do you build up or tear down?
Are you encouraging, compassionate, available to listen and discuss?
Or are you judgmental, ignoring, or just too busy?

People who are starting to grow spiritually are going to be attacked
by Satan. He is not going to want this growth to continue. Just as
a sapling cannot grow in the shade of a "bigger and better" tree a
baby Christian cannot grow in the shadow of someone who judges,
condescends, or doesn't have the time. Romans 3:12 states, "All
have turned away, they have together become worthless; there is
no one who does good, not even one." Satan will use insecurities to
stunt spiritual growth, don't be what he uses. In reading this, try to
examine your actions and intentions. Don't use others past mistakes,
lack of education of the Bible or all things "religious," background,
or anything else as an excuse not to be there for someone who
is searching. Are you used by God to build people up or are you used
by Satan to tear people down?

๏ะ ๕ะ

August 29

Our Stuff

One's life does not consist in the abundance of
the things he possesses. - Luke 12:15

I never seem to think I have enough stuff. I have many pairs of shoes, but when I look in my closet, I don't see a pair that seems "just right." I have several channels to watch, but find myself thinking, "There's nothing on TV tonight." I have a cabinet, freezer, and refrigerator full of food, but look and think, "I don't have anything to eat." Is it because in worldly terms, there is never enough?

We can possess a lot of things, but never seem satisfied. We can have a house full of stuff, and still want more. But, we have just one Jesus and He is always "just right." He is always enough. He can bring us joy and peace and love whether we are a "have" or a "have not" in this world. Our lives don't consist of our stuff, if our lives are focused on Him and He will never leave us wanting. With Him we are full!

August 30

Put to the Test

The tempter came to Him and said, "If you are the Son of
God, tell those stones to become bread." - Matthew 4:3

In this passage of scripture, Jesus had just fasted for forty day and
forty nights and he was hungry. Satan came to tempt Him, telling
Him if He was hungry to make the stones into bread. Jesus answered
him by saying, "Man does not live on bread alone, but on every
word that comes from the mouth of God" (Matthew 4:4). Satan
took Jesus up on a mountain and continued, "If you are the Son of
God, throw yourself down," going on to say that the angels would
come to save him (Matthew 4:5-6). Jesus responded, "Do not put
the Lord to a test" (Matthew 4:7). Jesus continued to repel Satan, so
he eventually left Him.

As I was reading this passage, I realized that, at times, I have done
the same thing to God. In sorrow I have said, "If you really loved
me, this wouldn't have happened." In arrogance and ignorance I
have said, "If I do this for you, then will you do this for me?" In
anger and self-pity I have said, "That's not fair!" Am I forgetting
who I am talking too? He showed me all He needed to at the cross.
Showing me that He loves me. Showing me what He would do for
me. And showing me with Him having to pay the price I owed, that
sometimes, life isn't fair. Jesus has already been put to the test, and
He passed!

Fatal Misunderstanding

In reply Jesus declared, "I tell you the truth, no one can see the kingdom of God unless he is born again." "How can a man be born when he is old?" Nicodemus asked. "Surely he cannot enter a second time into his mother's womb to be born!" - John 3:3-4

"Born again" here simply means "born from above." Can it be explained any better than that? This is an internal change that creates a new being. Nicodemus, a Pharisee and teacher, came to understand this symbolic message that Jesus was telling him. Jesus was figuratively speaking a spiritual truth. Just as in the telling of parables to the masses, Jesus was speaking in a language that Nicodemus could understand.

Without the understanding that only the Holy Spirit can provide, our faith in Jesus would never make any sense. This is why it's so impossible to witness to an unbeliever that is not being called by Him. It's only when He comes in to open the hearts and minds of the lost, can He be found.

I'm so glad that I was chosen to understand. I'm so thankful that I believe that he was born of a virgin, walked on water, and rose from the dead. Without a belief in all of these unbelievable things, I would be lost forever in my fatal misunderstanding!

September 1

Give it Another Try

When he had finished speaking, He said to Simon(Peter),
"Put out into deep water, and let down the nets for a catch."
Simon answered, "Master, we've worked hard all night and
haven't caught anything. But because you say so, I will let down
the nets." When they had done so, they caught such a large
number of fish that the nets began to break. - Luke 5:4-6

Have you ever worked hard at something with no results? Have you
ever said, "Well, I might as well give up!"? These fishermen in Luke
had worked all night and had nothing to show from it. Their nets
were empty. When Jesus said for them to "give it another try," they
came back with abundance!

We have all tried and failed at something. Some have worked on
a relationship, having nothing to show but frustration. Some have
worked on a career, only to see others climb the ladder. Some have
worked on themselves, accomplishing nothing but a deeper fall into
addiction, anger or depression. Bring Jesus into your plight, and
when He says, "give it another try," do as Peter did and say,
"Because You said so, I will!"

॰ಲ಄ ಄ಲ॰

September 2

A Sling and a Stone

So David prevailed over the Philistine with a
sling and a stone. - 1 Samuel 17:50

One night, a friend's young son was telling me the story of David and Goliath. I was so blessed by this five-year-old telling me the exciting details of this ancient story. Many have always known that David killed Goliath, but this story is so much more than that. This wasn't just a story about a boy killing a giant with a sling shot; it was about what you can accomplish when you trust in God. As the giant, Goliath, was laughing at his challenger, David said to him, "You come to me with a sword, with a spear, and with a javelin. But I come to you in the name of the Lord of hosts, the God of the armies of Israel, whom you have defied" (1 Samuel 17:45). Through human strength, David was no match for Goliath; but with God's strength, David was unbeatable!

We all have Goliath's in our lives. We see issues, problems, and hardships that we are no match for. If we could have the confidence of young David, who came through a fearful crowd to stand up and fight, we would beat the odds. If we could say, as David said, "You've come at me with everything you've got, but you know what? I have God and He's all I need!" Trust God to bring you through. Lean on Him when you need strength. And when you face your giants, grab your sling and a stone!

September 3

Humble Yourself

Whoever exalts himself will be humbled and he who
humbles himself will be exalted. - Matthew 23:12

One night, I was teaching my girls (11th and 12th grade girls) at church about humility. Tough subject! Like other commandments of Jesus, such as love and forgiveness, humility takes trust, obedience, and discipline.

The Bible tells us that "whoever exalts himself will be humbled and he who humbles himself will be exalted" (Matthew 23:12). This is the opposite of what our human nature tells us do. We are supposed to put our best foot forward. We are supposed to outshine the competition. We are supposed to get the upper hand. This world does not teach us that being humble will get you anywhere!

I was also asking the girls to think of someone that they thought of as humble. To be honest, I had to think a while! When my person finally popped into my mind, I was hit by a thought - that person is also one of the most peaceful people I know. Then, "God resists the proud, but gives grace to the humble" (1 Peter 5:5, James 4:6) came to my mind.

Humble people aren't selfish people, so they aren't as disappointed when things don't go exactly their way or work out best for them. Maybe if we managed to humble ourselves, the stresses of this world would not be as burdensome to us. If this happens, we wouldn't have to put ourselves on a pedestal - He will lift us up!

September 4

Let There Be Light

Then God said, "Let there be light," and there was light. - Genesis 1:3

During the Creation, God saw that there was only darkness in the world. He knew that wouldn't do, so He said, "Let there be light." He knew that we wouldn't be able to see our surroundings, to find our way, to see danger approaching - not without light.

Have you had a "Let there be light" moment in your life? I have. There was a time of darkness in my life. I couldn't always make out my surroundings. I couldn't find my way out. I definitely couldn't see danger approaching. God came in and said, "Let there be light" and with His help, I found my way out of the darkness.

What are the dark places in your life? Where do you need His light to shine in? Ask Him to come in today and say, "Let there be light!"

September 5

Come to Him

You are God, ready to pardon, precious and merciful, slow to anger, abundant in kindness. - Nehemiah 9:17

We have an amazing God! I sometimes find it very hard to comprehend the qualities He posses. It is hard for my human mind to grasp that these qualities can even exist at all. "Ready to pardon" - He is always ready to forgive me when I come to Him and ask. "Gracious and merciful" - His grace and mercy have helped me move past and move on to a better life in Him. "Slow to anger" - His patience with me is immeasurable. "Abundant in kindness" - When I stop to count my blessing, I will realize that my cup runs over!

Our God is not a dictator on a throne. He is a loving Father that can help us with any need. Do you seek forgiveness? Come to Him. Do you long for the grace and mercy that you can't seem to find in this world? Come to Him. Do you need someone that is patient and not quick tempered? Come to Him. Do you need kindness? Come to Him. Do you get the picture?

He Carries Us Home

And when he finds it, he joyfully puts it on his shoulders and goes home. - Luke 15:5

In the Parable of the Lord Sheep (Luke 15:3-7), Jesus talks about how a shepherd will leave his flock to look for just one sheep that is lost. He won't stop looking until he finds it. When he does find it, he carries it home and rejoices in its safe return. You might think, "Why does he care so much for this one sheep? Doesn't he have 99 more?" Each is important to him.

This parable goes on to say, "I tell you that in the same way, there will be more rejoicing in Heaven over one sinner who repents than over 99 righteous persons who do not need to repent." Jesus loves all of us, we are His sheep. He will search for the one who has strayed, the one who is in trouble, the one who need Him. He will not leave you behind saying, "Oh well, lost that one, but I have more."

No matter how far you have strayed, He can find you. No matter what kind of trouble you have gotten yourself into, He can help you. No matter how upside down you have gotten in this world, He can set you right side up. This Shepherd will not stop until all of His sheep are safe at home!

September 7

Tree or Twig?

He is like a tree planted beside streams of water that bears its fruit in season and whose leaf does not wither. Whatever he does prospers. - Psalm 1:3

Did you know that the "General Sherman" Sequoia tree is the largest living thing in the world? They are so massive that one single tree could build around 120 average size homes. These trees have a massive root system, so deeply anchored in the ground, that storm after storm can come through, and they will still be standing when the clouds clear. Scripture tells us, "He will be like a tree planted by water; it sends its roots out toward a stream, it doesn't fear when heat comes, and its foliage remain green. It will not worry in a year of drought or cease producing fruit" (Jeremiah 17:8).

This made me start to wonder, "How deep are my roots?" When the storms of life roll through, am I going to stand tall like the giant Sequoia or am I going to be uprooted like a twig? The answer comes from another question, "How is my relationship with Jesus?" I guess the answer to that will tell me which kind of tree I really am!

September 8

Hearing Him

Speak, Lord, for Your servant hears. – 1 Samuel 3:9

The words in the above verse are words I want to hear myself say daily. I want to be willing and available to Him at all times. I want this, but I don't always do it. What gets in my way? Well, that list can differ every day. I don't intentionally ignore God, but I know that sometimes I do. I think my biggest problem is that sometimes I don't stop long enough to listen.

Studying His Word helps us to know God. Spending time with Him in prayer helps us grow closer to God. Don't stop there! Stay with Him long enough to listen. Soon you might find yourselves saying, "Speak, Lord, for Your servant hears!"

September 9

Change is Possible

So he, trembling and astonished, said, "Lord,
what do You want me to do?" - Acts 9:6

Before his Damascus Road conversion, Paul helped in persecuting the Christians. In Acts 22:20 he admits, "And when the blood of Your martyr Stephen was shed, I was standing by consenting to his death, and guarding the clothes of those who were killing him." Even though in Paul's past he committed heinous acts, this is not what he is remembered for. He is remembered as the Apostle Paul, a man dedicated to and know for spreading the Gospel of Christ, of great discipline and faith, and that many after him strived to be. Paul changed and never looked back. He didn't let his past stop his future. He went from being the persecutor of Jesus to being persecuted for Jesus. He changed everything!

We sometimes wonder if we can change. Remember the old saying, "You can't teach an old dog new tricks?" This doesn't apply when you have Jesus. Change is possible. Hope can be found. Faith will be renewed. This happens everyday! You just have to be like Paul and say, "Lord, what do you want me to do?" The past is finished, the present can be changed, and the future is what you make it. Make it for Him!

September 10

In the Red

He Himself is the propitiation for our sins. - 1 John 2:2

Have you ever looked at your monthly bills coming in and thought, "How will I ever pay all of this?" Do you look at your income to debt ratio and see that there is no way? If we got monthly statements listing our sins like a credit card statement, we would all just have to file spiritual bankruptcy.

In the past, when all accounting records used to be handwritten, if you were in debt, they would write your totals in red ink. If you were out of debt, they would right them in black ink. Without Christ, there would never be any way for you to get out of the red. So, we have to look to another red, the blood of Christ.

The word "propitiation" means appeasement or satisfaction. The death of Christ on the cross satisfied the demand of a punishment for sin, not His, but ours. His mercy to us and His faithfulness to God paid our debt. One that we could never have paid for ourselves. In looking at the accounting records of your spiritual life, are you in the red?

September 11

False Teachers

In their greed these teachers will exploit you with stories they have made up. Their condemnation has long been hanging over them, and their destruction has not been sleeping. - 2 Peter 2:3

Today, September 11, reminds us of the power of false teaching. The hijackers that took so many lives that day in 2001, including their own, believed in what they were doing. They had probably been brought up since birth for this cause they carried out. They had been lied to and manipulated. They had been sentenced to an eternity in torment, and they didn't even realize it. So much pain for so many people, all because of false teaching.

Jesus commanded us to "Go, therefore and make disciples of all nations, baptizing them in the name of the Father and of the Son and of the Holy Spirit" (Matthew 28:19). These false teachers are not going to stop spreading lies, so we can never stop spreading the truth!

ᏺᏫᏺ

September 12

The Comfort of Jesus

Now there was leaning on Jesus' bosom one of His
disciples, whom Jesus loved. - John 13:23

In this passage of scripture, Jesus knew that His time on this earth was coming to an end. This was the time when Jesus told the disciples that one of them would betray Him. The disciples were all confused and upset. John, often called "the disciple whom Jesus loved," was leaning against Jesus. I think John was letting his weariness, his sorrow, and his confusion wash away in Him. To me, this is a beautiful and vivid picture of the comfort we can receive from Christ.

When we are confused and upset, we can lean on Jesus. We can be comforted by Him at any time. We can have peace, His peace, inside our hearts. Trouble will come, but He can make it better!

ﻬ ﻬ

September 13

Trust and Faith

When I am afraid, I put my trust in you. - Psalm 56:3

This passage seems like it should be simple to do, right? If so, then why don't we actually do what it says? I know that sometimes when we are completely stressed out, extremely afraid, or tired of worrying about something that we finally think to go to God. Why don't we do that in the first place? Is it because at first it seems like it's not a big deal? Is it because it's something we think we can handle on our own? Or is it because we have gotten out of the habit of turning to Him? There are a lot of reasons why we have to not put our faith and trust in God.

What I have found is that when I trust Him and put my faith in Him, that is when my problems don't seem so impossible, my heartbreak doesn't seem so devastating, and my fears don't seems so scary! Let's try to make it our first instinct to run to Him!

God's Word

In the beginning was the Word, and the Word was
with God, and the Word was God. – John 1:1

I was thinking about "Reality TV." Do you make sure you are home for it? Do you have it listed in your DVR recordings? People seem to love reality TV.

I started comparing those TV shows to Biblical stories. For those who watch "The Amazing Race", they need to read about the Israelites fleeing Egypt and the Red Sea parting at just the right time. For those who watch "Fear Factor", they need to read about Shadrach, Mechach, and Abed-Nego who had to deny God or face a fiery furnace. For those who watch "Survivor", they need to read about the Israelites roaming in the wilderness for years waiting to enter the Promised Land.

God's Word not only gives us love, support, counsel, and direction; it also gives us wonderful stories of real life heroes who were faithful to Him. We make sure we don't miss our weekly reality TV. Let's also make sure spending time reading and studying God's Word is just as important!

September 15

Which Shoulder?

When tempted, no one should say, "God is tempting me." For God cannot be tempted by evil, nor does He tempt anyone. - James 1:13

You shouldn't ever have to question where temptation comes from. We've all seen the cartoons where the angel sits on one shoulder encouraging good and the devil sits on the other coaxing evil. Every difficult situation in the life of a Christian either strengthens his faith or allows him to fall. But, God isn't the one tempting you. God's nature has no capacity or vulnerability to evil.

Just as in the story of Job, God allows trials to occur and through them can come temptation. He has also promised that we will not be left without an alternative choice (1 Cor. 10:13). Whether we escape or give in depends on us. If you were a cartoon, which shoulder would you listen too?

September 16

The Widow's Offering

"I tell you the truth," Jesus said, "this poor widow has
given more than all the rest of them. For they have
given a tiny part of their surplus, but she, poor as she
is, has given everything she has." – Luke 21:3-4

In this story in Luke, we see that there are some that trusted in Jesus completely. That there were some who gave all they have. Did you notice that it was this poor widow that did it? Did you notice that she, not knowing where she would get her next meal, gave Jesus all she had?

When was the last time you gave Jesus all you had? I'm not talking about only money here. Although, giving monetary offerings to Jesus is an act of obedience that we should do, and should want to do, but I'm talking about "everything you have." Money is one part of giving of yourself, but what about your time? What about your heart? Is your heart given wholly to Jesus? What part have you kept to yourself? What we give in abundance externally shows what we have given in abundance internally. Have you given Him all you have?

September 17

Christ is Truth

> Then we will no longer be immature like children. We won't
> be tossed and blown about by every wind of new teaching.
> We will not be influenced when people try to trick us with
> lies so clever they sound like the truth. – Ephesians 4:14

It seems like, in today's times, the word "God" has become a generic term. You can say God without a glance from others, but to say Jesus Christ, gets feathers ruffled. "Religion" is a bad word, but "spiritual" is accepted. It's no longer about who God is, but about what this word represents. People are getting more and more confused by these thoughts circulating in society.

As Christians, we must be very careful and aware. We need to make sure we study God's Word. We need to know the truth so we can spot the false. We need to spend time with Him is prayer. We need to seek His strength and not conform to this new way of thinking. You won't be confused by others when you are following the words of Christ!

Have Faith

Just then a woman who had been subject to bleeding for twelve years came up behind him and touched the edge of his cloak. She said to herself, "If I only touch his cloak, I will be healed." - Matthew 9:20-21

This woman who is mentioned here in the Gospel of Matthew was an outcast in her society. She had an ailment that kept her shunned for 12 years. She, knowing Christ was near, braved the maddening crowd to make her way to be close to him. She braved a crowd that didn't think she was fit to be in their presence, a crowd that saw her as "unclean." Why did she do this? She did this because she had faith.

If we fight our way through this world that condemns, judges, disapproves, and come to Jesus; we will be made whole. Our problem may not be externally as was the case with this woman in scripture. Our problem may be on the inside. In the end of this story, Jesus turned to her and said, "Take heart, daughter, your faith has healed you" (Matthew 9:22). Be brave and have faith. Let His healing take place in you!

September 19

Pray Without Ceasing

Pray without ceasing. - 1 Thessalonians 5:17

I used to read this verse and think, "How can I possibly pray without ceasing?" If I prayed constantly, how would I ever get anything else done? I didn't understand how that could possible be right, but this is scripture, so I had to be missing something. I was actually picturing, in my mind, being at home, kneeling down beside my bed and praying. In that picture, it's not possible to "pray without ceasing."

What I realized is that being in constant prayer is not about a pose or position, but a state of mind. It is about keeping Jesus close to me at all times. In good times, be in prayer (rejoice in Him). In bad times, be in prayer (draw Him close). In the everyday, be in prayer (keep Him close). This, of course, is my uneducated opinion, but it helps me understand that "praying without ceasing" is more than just kneeling beside my bed and having a quite moment with my Savior. It's about involving Him in my life and keeping Him close!

ೲ ೯ೲ

September 20

Waiting for an Answer

My soul, wait silently for God alone, for my
expectation is from Him. - Psalm 62:5

I am not a very patient person and I'm sure I share that characteristic with many others. We live in a society where we usually can get what we want when we want it. We can get food a few minutes after ordering what we want to eat. We can get gas in our vehicles quickly because there are gas stations on every corner. We can change the channel on the TV with a press of a button. We don't have to wait for much.

Waiting on an answer to prayer is never easy. There are things I have been praying about for years that I still don't have an answer to. There are crucial things, like a biopsy my mother had, that we had to wait a week to find out the results. I didn't want to wait to find out whether or not my mother was going to be okay. The truth is, I don't like waiting for anything. But, maybe God has me wait in order for me to put my trust in Him and completely put my requests in His capable hands.

Whether it's, "Should I take a new job or stay with the one I have now?", "Is my loved one going to be okay?", "Should I marry this person?", or "Please Lord, something is wrong with my child, what can I do?" We all have questions to which we want answers. God doesn't work like a remote control. He has His timing and will let us know the answers when the time comes. What we need to do is keep praying, keep asking, and trust that He will answer.

September 21

What Are You Saying?

Let your conversation be gracious and attractive so that you
will have the right response for everyone. - Colossians 4:4

I was sitting at a public picnic table with my nieces one day. We were
just sitting there killing time, waiting on my brother. At the table
next to us, there was a group of people that looked to be in their late
teens to early twenties. As I sat waiting, these kids proceeded to say
the most awful things and using foul language. My nieces were in
plain sight! There was no way these kids didn't see them. They just
didn't seem to care.

When young, impressionable children are around, take notice. Jesus
said, "Let the little children come to me, and do not hinder them, for
the kingdom of heaven belongs to such as these" (Matthew 19:14).
Don't let your conversations be a hindrance to anyone. Watch what
you say in the presence of strangers. As a Christian, you are on
display. Don't let your conversations be something parents cringe
when their children overhear!

September 22

Everything We Need

Come, all you who are thirsty, come to the waters; and you
who have no money, come, buy and eat! Come, buy wine
and milk without money and without cost. - Isaiah 55:1

Some times, when I go to the grocery store, it's one of those rush trips I do so often when I decide to cook something specific that particular night. Other times, I go and get everything I think I might need for the next week or so. During these trips, usually, when I check out, the total is bigger than I would have guessed it would be. Getting what we need in this life always comes at a cost.

In the above verse, "come, buy wine and milk" is symbolic of abundance or satisfaction. Then it goes on to say, "without money and without cost" shows how through Christ's sacrifice, there is no cost because it has already been paid. Simply put, we can get everything we need through Jesus for free!

୬୧୧ ୨୭୬

September 23

Motion Sickness

The path of the righteous is level; O upright One, you
make the way of the righteous smooth. - Isaiah 26:7

I tend to suffer from motion sickness. When I was little, and we
would go on a trip, there would come a time that we would have
to pull over on the side on the road because I would get sick. Even
now, when I'm traveling, I just close my eyes and try to sleep through
it. In my opinion, this is one of the worst feelings. Why? Because I
can't make it stop.

We can also suffer from emotional motion sickness. We can feel like
life is taking one curvy road after another. We might feel like we are
turning green and can't just close our eyes and hope to sleep through
it. The prophet Isaiah wrote the above verse. It's the motion sickness
remedy for our lives. The Hebrew word for "uprightness" means
"straight." So, even in a world of hilly, twisted roads, the "upright
One", Jesus, if we trust Him, can make our path straight. Do you
suffer from motion sickness? Look to Jesus!

September 24

The Full Picture

I delight to do Your will, my God; Your instruction
resides within me. – Psalm 40:8

One time, I messed up the picture on my TV. Somehow, I made it smaller. The picture was no longer 32", but was maybe around 28." I wanted to see the full picture. I fumbled with the remote, pushing every button I saw. I finally got frustrated and gave up. But, I never once thought about getting the instruction manual to see how to fix it. Does that make sense? Not really. But, don't we sometimes do the same thing in our spiritual life.

A question a lot of people ask is, "What's God's will for me?" We spend effort and time thinking about what we think God wants from us. All we have to do is pick up the Bible. The Bible tells us what is expected of us and about the promises of God. It explains to us what God's will is for our lives. And if we are confused, we have the Holy Spirit within us to guide our way. So, if you want to see the full picture, get out the instruction manual!

ഐ ഈ

September 25

Who Will Say Thank You?

I know. I know your deeds, your hard work,
your perseverance. – Revelation 2:2

On my way to work one morning, I heard an older song titled, "Thank You." It is a song about a man who died and went to Heaven. When he got there, there were a line of people waiting to say thank you. Numerous people wanting to tell him how he, in some way, played a part in getting them there. Whether it was him teaching Sunday School, or giving money to a missionary, he had done so many things for God and for His purpose. I cry every time I hear that song. It always makes me think of what I have done or not done to get others into Heaven. This fictional man did not expect a thank you for the things he had done, but was touched all the same.

I don't think we realize what a kind word, a moment spent, or money given can do. Without God, it might not do anything, but with Him and if your heart is right, the outcomes are endless. I urge you today to be aware of what you do, how you treat those around you, and to be looking for an opportunity to be of service to God. Your life and how you live it is either promoting Him or hindering Him. Which one are you?

His Peace

Peace I leave with you, My peace I give to you; not as
the world gives do I give to you. Let not your heart be
troubled, neither let it be afraid. – John 14:27

How many times have you felt peaceful? How many times have
you let the peace of the Holy Spirit flow through you? Sometimes
when the world is getting to me, I stop and close my eyes and allow
His peace to come in. If I waited on my peace, I would never have
any. I would be too caught up in what I could be doing, how unfair
something is, or how to keep myself busy so I don't have to think
about what's bothering me. Peace, this kind of peace, comes only
from Jesus. He is the only one who can calm our storms and settle
us down.

Jesus promised the Holy Spirit would come and live in us. We have
the power of God inside us, but I'm not sure we use it very often.
If you are like me, I sometimes wait until I am so worked up, sad,
angry, or utterly confused before I seek His peace, His patience, or
His guidance. I don't need to wait. The instant something happens
I need to go to Him. Jesus said, "Peace I leave with you, My peace
I give to you" – stop, close your eyes, and allow His peace to come
in!

Give and Take

With the same measure that you use, it will be
measured back to you. - Luke 6:38

In most cases, in human relationships, in order to receive something, you have to give something. To receive love, you must be willing to give love. To receive friendship, you must be willing to be a friend. To receive forgiveness, you must be able to forgive others. All of these things are a give and take kind of relationship. You must do your part!

On the other side, if you judge, you will be judged as well. If you are hard on people, they will probably be hard on you. If you are proud, or condescending, or greedy; all these things can and will turn on you.

Jesus said, "Love your neighbor as yourself" (Matthew 22:39). The measure we want others to use in treating us, needs to be the measure we use in how we treat others. You aren't a special case, this applies to everyone. Pray that God shows you how to give what it is that you would like to receive.

Following the Blind

*"If a blind man leads a blind man, both will
fall into a pit." – Matthew 15:14*

In this passage of Scripture, Jesus is talking bout the Scribes and Pharisees. He called them "blind guides." They put on a religious front, but they had evil in their hearts. There are many blind guides out there today. Whether it is favorite authors, TV or local pastors, celebrities, family, or friends, make sure your spiritual mentors are seeking their guidance from God's Word. Make sure they guide you follow is Jesus. Make sure you are following Him and not the world. If you are following any path but His, you will blindly fall into a pit.

The world says it's okay to do this and do that. If it feels good do it. Do what makes you happy. The world is building an "it's all about you" generation. The world turns a blind eye to many things that God's Word does not. The Bible tells us that "no one can serve two masters." You follow His path or you follow the world's path. These paths do not follow the same road. Don't follow the blind guides; it's only through Him that you truly receive sight!

September 29

What's Good?

Clearly no one is justified before God by the law, because,
"The righteous will live by faith. – Galatians 3:11

Several years ago, I had a friend who told me that he didn't think
God would send any good person to hell. What makes someone
good? I knew him well and there are some in society who would not
have viewed him as good, but to those around him, he was. He didn't
murder, or steal, or commit any other heinous crime, but there were
some things he did do that others might see as "bad." We all have
different ideas of what is "good" or "bad," but the Bible tells us that
"there is no one who does good, not even one" (Romans 3:12).

I think this misconception of "I'm not going to hell because I'm a
good person" might send more people there than anything else. I'm
sorry to say, I didn't correct my friend when he said this and I have
thought of him many times since. I didn't know exactly what to say,
I was afraid of how he might respond, and now that opportunity
might not ever come again. My prayer is that I will be bold and be
prepared for those who question. My prayer is that I will be able to
share God's Word when an opportunity presents itself. Definitions
of good and bad don't really matter because there is only one way
to Heaven and that is Jesus. It's up to those who know to tell those
who don't!

Using the Unlikely

Mordecai had a cousin named Hadassah, whom he had brought up because she had neither father nor mother. This girl, who was also known as Esther, was lovely in form and features, and Mordecai had taken her as his own daughter when her father and mother died. - Esther 2:7

I took a Bible study on Esther at my church. While studying the part of how Esther became queen of Persia, I also thought about other royal weddings I've witnessed in my lifetime. The most famous, of course, was Charles and Diana. Diana came from nobility. She had been groomed since birth to become a queen. Not Esther, she was an orphaned, Jewish girl, living in a pagan nation, who had been raised by a single man. See what happens when God has a plan?

Esther was an unlikely queen with an amazing destiny. She saved her race from extinction. She was an ordinary girl with an extraordinary path, and a scary path. She became willing to give her own life if necessary to save her people. She is never mentioned with the patriarchs of great faith, so she was probably just a normal girl who believed and God grew her unselfish faith from that.

God can work miracles in each of our lives. He can make the ordinary, extraordinary. He can make the weak, strong. He can take those who believe and grow a great faith. He can take the unlikely and make them a queen!

October 1

Temptation Awaits

When the devil had finished tempting Jesus, he left Him until the next opportunity came. – Luke 4:13

I know sometimes I think I'm the only one who suffers with this or that. We are naturally self-centered and think this way. I have had others tell me that there are temptations today that were not there in the past. Temptation now is too strong. We are too weak. Hebrews tells us, "For we do not have a High Priest who is unable to sympathize with our weakness, but we have One who has been tempted in every way, just as we are – yet was without sin" (Hebrews 4:15).

Sin is not new and human weakness isn't either. Satan's tricks are not new. We are blessed in that Our God is not new to our struggle either. He was here in the beginning and will be here until the end. Look to Him to fight the temptations in your life. Lean on Him for strength and endurance. Jesus told us, "I have told you these things, so that in me you may have peace. In this world you will have trouble. But take heart! I have overcome the world" (John 16:33)!

He Is Here

We will find grace to help us when we need it. – Hebrews 4:16

When I was little, when I thought of God, I always pictured this grand-fatherly figure sitting on a throne high above in Heaven. I never thought this was a bad or skewed depiction of Him. I just thought that was where He was. Up there, not down here.

As I got older, and not always doing what was best, I didn't like to think of God being here with me. I didn't like to think about the fact that He could see everything I was doing. Denial was keeping my eyes closed, not His.

Now, I realize how blessed I am to have Him with me. At any time, all I have to do is turn to Him and He's right there! He's not up in Heaven just watching the show. He's not turning a blind eye to my disobedience. He's with me, no matter where I am or what I'm doing. He's ready and willing to help when I need Him. Isn't that amazing! His grace is sufficient for me, and for you!

Have You Lost Your Luster?

Make me know thy ways, O Lord; teach me Thy paths.
Lead me in thy truth and teach me. – Psalm 25:4-5

I had written this verse on a card and taped it to my bathroom mirror. Over time, the card became curled and dirty, and probably has some hairspray on it. What bothered me is that I couldn't pin point at what time I stopped seeing it. I guess I just got so used to it being there that I no longer noticed it. When I realized this, it made me so sad. I was so excited when I put it on the mirror, and at some point, it was just something that took up space.

I got to thinking about those times in our walk with Christ that at first, are so exciting, then, in time, lose their luster. Why do you think this happens? Why can we be so excited to discover something new about God only to find contentment in it, ultimately letting it fade? God's Word and all that has to do with Him never loses its luster, so the fade must be within us. Spending time studying God's word keeps you learning from Him daily. Spending time with God in prayer keeps your faith from becoming cold or stale. Praising God keeps worship from becoming a habit or routine. Making sure you pay attention to your relationship with God keeps you on the right path.

Don't let music become sound instead of praise. Don't let the sermon become noise instead of a message. Don't let the verses you read become just knowledge instead of a lesson or a promise. Don't let the verse you put on the mirror fade into the background. Don't lose your luster for God. Be a light in the darkness for Him!

Blessed Assurance

And the God of all grace, who called you to his eternal glory in Christ, after you have suffered a little while, will himself restore you and make you strong, firm and steadfast. - 1 Peter 5:10

When people share with me that they or a loved one of theirs is going through a tough time, I immediately start looking up some scripture and some songs to share with them. The above verse is one of my favorite "tough time" verses. The problem is that sometimes those who are going through a tough time don't have any faith. If there isn't any faith in Jesus, then scripture and songs are going to do much help. They might think, "Well, that's a nice thought, but….." This is were we have a good opportunity to witness to them, but I also take just a moment to be thankful for myself.

In thinking about this, the hymn "Blessed Assurance" came to my mind. "Blessed assurance, Jesus is mine." Thank you Jesus! I can't imagine having to go through any tough time without Him. Do you know someone going through a tough time with no "blessed assurance" to hold on to? Let's lift up some prayers for them today!

~ogleol gleo~

How to Pray

Be serious and watchful in your prayers. - 1 Peter 4:7

When you get to be an adult, you think you know how to pray. In some ways, I've come a long way from the entire year I prayed for a swimming pool when I was a little. In other ways, I'm still just a selfish child.

I was thinking and examining how I pray. I thought about how I pray for myself, my family, and my friends. In looking at different references to prayer in the Bible, we can find many guides on how to pray. It's usually not about prayer alone! "Be anxious for nothing, but in everything by prayer and supplication, with thanksgiving, let your requests be made known to God" (Philippians 4:6). "Confess your trespasses to one another, and pray for one another, that you may be healed. The effective, fervent prayer of a righteous man avails much" (James 5:16). "We will give ourselves continually to prayer and to the ministry of the word" (Acts 6:4). There are many other references, but you get the point. Prayer is not just an action in itself. It's a way of living that goes along with walking with the Lord. Seeking His will. Studying His word and His way. It's about being in sync with Him! It's about having faith and trust in Him.

I have realized that I may not be asking for a swimming pool anymore, but I'm not always using my prayer time for what it's truly meant to be. It's meant to be a part of my walk with God. I need to start everyday saying, "Lord, teach me to pray" (Luke 11:1)!

Our Strength

The godly may trip seven times, but they will get up again. But one disaster is enough to overthrow the wicked. - Proverbs 24:16

If any of you are like me, you have tripped and fell many times. Isn't it wonderful to know that, with Jesus, you have what it takes to get up and keep going? The Holy Spirit within you is strength in your weakness, wisdom in your ignorance, and conscience when you are drifting.

Non-believers think that this life is it. This is as good as it is going to ever get for them. Maybe that is why it is such an unrecoverable disaster for this life not to go as they have planned. As believers, we can rise up when we fall because we have something that is stronger than this world. Jesus said, "In this world you will have trouble. But take heart! I have overcome the world" (John 16:33). We have something that is bigger than any success or failure we may have. We have Jesus!

Do You Have Deep Roots?

The seed on rocky soil represents those who hear the message and immediately receive it with joy. But since they don't have deep roots, they don't last long. They fall away as soon as they have problems or are persecuted for believing God's Word. - Matthew 13:20-21

In the "Parable of the Farmer Scattering Seed" (Matthew 13:1-23), Jesus talks about the different reactions to hearing God's Word. Some hear it and understand it, some don't. Some hear it and get excited about it, yet others just let it fade. Then there are those where the message sets in and grows into something wonderful and meaningful. There are many examples in this parable, which one is describing you?

Keep your excitement of being in and learning from God's word. Cherish it because it was given for you. Learn from it and come to know what God's will is. Don't be like the seeds that got eaten by birds, burned up by the sun, or choked by weeds and thorns. Be like the seeds on good soil that grew deep roots. Those are the seeds that will someday bear fruit!

Give Yourself

Peter said, "I don't have any silver or gold for you. But I'll give you what I have. In the name of Jesus Christ, get up and walk!" - Acts 3:6

I was incredibly moved by Peter's words here, "I'll give you what I have." He meant those words. He lived to and died for spreading the Good News of Jesus Christ. He didn't have riches. He didn't have an education. He didn't have the status of the Sadducess. Without all of this, he will still be remembered throughout history as a devout follower and disciple of Jesus Christ.

When you come to Jesus and want to live your life for Him, He doesn't expect anything you don't have. All He wants to hear is, "I'll give you what I have - I'll give you me." I promise that will be enough!

October 9

Talk to Him

Love is patient and kind. - I Corinthians 13:4

Once, while spending a Sunday afternoon with a friend of mine and her son, she was having a hard time trying to figure out what was wrong with him and he was really fussy. He was at the age where he could say a few words, but he was just crying and fussing. With patience only a mother can have, she said, "Use your words, and tell me what is wrong. I can help you if you will talk to me."

I got to thinking about what she had said. God's love for us is so patient and so kind. He wants us to tell Him what's wrong. He want's us to come to Him and talk to Him. Even through, and unlike my friend, God already knows what is wrong; He is waiting for us to tell Him. Ask for His help. He, like my friend to her son, is saying, "Use your words, and tell me what is wrong. I can help you if you will talk to me."

October 10

Kingdom of Heaven

"Repent, for the kingdom of Heaven is at hand." – Matthew 4:17

In every movie you see where it looks like the world is going to be destroyed, you will usually see a crazy looking, homeless person carrying a sign that says, "Repent, for the kingdom of Heaven is at hand." I always laugh at the fact that (1) some in Hollywood must think that only a crazy looking, homeless person would ever repent or believe in God, and (2) the kingdom of Heaven is always at hand!

This was not a phrase that Hollywood came up with; these were Jesus' own words. When He began to preach and to fulfill the words of Isaiah, "people living in darkness have seen a great light; on those living in the land of the shadow of death a light has dawned" (Matthew 4:16, Isaiah 9:1-2), He said, "Repent, for the kingdom of Heaven is at hand."

This, to me, was not an announcement of the end of the world, but an offer to have the full resources of the kingdom of Heaven with you at all times. God's strength, God's power, God's mercy and love, all of it – at your hands. Repent of your sins, chose Him as your Savior, have nothing getting in the way of having a relationship with God, and He will be with you. Without Him, you are no match for this world, but "He has overcome the world" (John 16:33). Some translations say, "the kingdom of Heaven is near," don't you think that means that Jesus, God Himself, was close and was with them? Don't let sin get in your way. Have Jesus near and have the kingdom of Heaven at hand!

ꙅꙉ ꙅꙉ

October 11

Doing His Business

Do Business Till I Come Back. - Luke 19:13

In the "Parable of the Ten Servants" in Luke 19, a nobleman leaves his home to travel and orders his servants to invest his money while he is gone. The servants that did well with what they were given received rewards. For those servants that didn't produce in his absence, all was taken away.

Jesus has left us with a job to do. We aren't just supposed to sit around and wait for Him to come back and take us home. We are supposed to increase His investment. His numbers are supposed to grow. We are supposed to spread His Word throughout the world. What kind of servant are you? Will you be one who hears, "Well done!" (Luke 19:17, 19) or will you hear, "You wicked servant!" (Luke 19:22)? Don't ever think that there is nothing for you to do. Don't ever think that you aren't smart enough, or talented enough, or knowledgeable enough to talk to someone about Christ. Willingness is all it takes, God gives you the words to say (John 14:26). He wants us to "do business till He comes back!"

Bad Company

Do not be misled: Bad company corrupts good
character. - 1 Corinthians 15:33

I have heard over and over again how it's okay to have close friends
that are not in fellowship with God. I have heard people say many
times, "Well, Jesus had dinner with sinners," or "Jesus loved and
accepted everyone." These are both very true statements, but should
not be used as justification for having close friends of questionable
character or who are living immoral lives. Don't misunderstand me,
you shouldn't shun anyone. I am talking about the people who are
close to you and with whom you spend a lot of time.

Jesus didn't bring into his inner circle anyone but the truly devoted.
Jesus didn't turn a blind eye to things that were not right. Jesus was
not around these people to "hang out." He was there to save!

October 13

Child-Like Kindness

*Kind words are like honey, sweet to the soul and
healthy for the body. - Proverb 16:24*

When our pastor was talking with our children about being kind to others, I caught myself thinking, "This is just as much a message to all the adults looking on." We all need to have a child-like kindness. Children have it easier sometimes because they have not yet been jaded, had too many huge disappointments, and no big failures have weakened their spirit. It is usually through life experiences, that our "unkindness" rears its ugly head.

Have you ever been unkind to someone that didn't deserve it? I have. Have you ever ignored someone in need? I have. Have you ever been too busy to care? Regretfully, I admit I have. So often, I have found myself longing for the child-like faith I see in the young children I am supposed to be teaching. Should I also long for child-like kindness?

Age seems to tarnish our kindness toward others. We stock our cabinets with anti-aging products for our outsides. Let's pay just as much attention to the inside. Remember the words of Paul to the Romans, "Be kind to one another" (Romans 12:10). Show kindness to someone today. Afterwards, you might find yourself skipping like a child with delight!

Foreign Land

How shall we sing the Lord's song in a foreign land? - Psalm 137:4

When I read this verse, my first thought was that this was for missionaries. People who go to other countries and other cultures trying to spread the Gospel of Christ. After pondering for a minute, I realized that this verse is for everyone. We don't live in a Christian bubble. Sometimes, a lot of the time, we are all in a foreign land, surrounded by the lost. So, how do we sing the Lords' song wherever we are?

No matter where we are, we don't need to forget who we are and more importantly - Whose we are. Unless you are in church or surrounded by your believing friends, it's not always easy to be a Christian. Our ways seem foreign to those who don't know Christ. I have even been called behind the times or needing to join the real world. This is a compliment to me because my Savior said, "I am not of this world" (John 8:23). So, I guess my point is - you don't have to be a missionary to enter a foreign land!

October 15

Getting What You Need

Your Father knows the things you have need of
before you ask Him. - Matthew 6:8

Have you ever really needed something and it just happened? The friend you share everything with just happens to call you when you are trying to solve a problem. The perfect song comes on the radio that describes the very feeling you are experiencing. The hug you get from a loved one for no apparent reason. These are all things you might have needed, but didn't necessarily plan on getting at that moment.

You have heard me say this before, but I'm going to say it again - God knows us! He knows what we need before we ask Him. If you are like me, I sometimes don't know what to ask for. I don't always know what it is that I need. Every morning I say, "God, please be with me throughout this day." He is there through my friend who calls at the perfect time. He is there through the song of praise to Him on the radio. He is there in that unexpected hug. Everyday I ask, not knowing what I will need that day, He is there and He is prepared!

288 | *Leigh Ann Madding*

⁖⊙⊙⊙⊙⊙

October 16

Lightening Won't Strike

So they went and entered the house of a prostitute
named Rahab and stayed there. - Joshua 2:1

I know all of you have heard someone say, "If I go into that church, lightening will strike!" Some feel they are just "too bad" of a person and beyond salvation. If you study many of the Bible stories, you will find that God often used "bad people" to do His will.

One great example is Rahab. She was a prostitute from Jericho. She had grown up in a pagan culture. She was not, as they say, "a girl you would bring home to Mamma!" But, she feared a Lord she didn't even know. She trusted two men who followed this Lord and helped them. She had faith that this Lord would save her and her family. Her life was changed by this trust and she was never the same again. The Bible tells us that, "Joshua spared Rahab the prostitute, with her family and all who belonged to her, because she hid the men Joshua had sent as spies to Jericho - and she lives among the Israelites to this day" (Joshua 6:25).

No one is "too bad" to save. There are no "lost causes" when it comes to the Lord. If you trust in Him and believe He will save you, it can and will happen. James tells us, "Was not even Rahab the prostitute considered righteous for what she did?" (James 2:25). Don't expect lightening to strike, just come as you are!

October 17

Praising God

I will praise the Lord at all times. I will constantly
speak His praises. - Psalm 34:1

In both good times and bad times, David would praise the Lord.
When he killed Goliath, he praised the Lord. When Saul was
trying to kill him, he praised the Lord. When he was anointed
King of Judah, he praised the Lord. When his son died, he praised
the Lord. His faith and love toward God never changed with his
circumstances.

David was called "a man after God's own heart" (1 Samuel 13:14,
Acts 13:22). Isn't that a great thing to be remembered for? When
we have trials and suffering, good news and accomplishments, don't
forget to praise the Lord. He can bring you through anything. He
can celebrate in your happiness. He is always there!

Tumbling Walls

And the seventh time it happened, when the priests blew
the trumpets, that Joshua said to the people: "Shout,
for the Lord has given you this city!" - Joshua 6:16

The fall of Jericho is a strange story. Joshua and his army didn't scale the wall and attack. They didn't wait for the people to come outside. They marched silently for 6 days. Why? Because that is what God told them to do. I'm sure some of the soldiers were thinking, "I wasn't trained for this! Let's get in there and show them that the stories they have heard about us are true!" Then, to make things more peculiar, the seventh day, they marched around Jericho's walls seven times. Really, this is getting ridiculous! But, on the seventh time, the Lord had told them to start shouting as loud as they could, and guess what? The walls came tumbling down!

God's plans may not always make sense to us. We might not understand or even like what's going on. During these confusing times, faith and trust are a must! We need to remember the words, "And we know that all things work together for good to those who love God, to those who are called according to His purpose" (Romans 8:28). You may be frustrated with the friend you have been witnessing to for ages. You may feel that your prayers on a certain subject will never be answered. You may feel that nothing you do makes any difference. If you feel like you are marching around in circles, just wait - the walls will come tumbling down!

October 19

Why Pray?

Men always ought to pray and not lose heart. - Luke 18:1

I remember buying my mother a coffee mug that had the saying "Why pray, when I can fret and worry?" I know, I not should make fun of my mother. Sorry Mom! It is human nature to worry. We all do it. And saying, "don't worry" is easier said than done. Or is it?

Why is it that our first tendency is to worry and our last tendency is to pray? When you tell someone you will pray for them, do you do it quickly so you won't forget? Do you wonder why you don't hear from God, but conveniently forget that you haven't even gone to Him with your problem? Do you use prayer as a last resort instead of a first line of defense? I have been guilty of all these things, have you? I think we should all give prayer a try. Let's see what happens!

ஒ௸ ௵

October 20

Share Your Laughter

Sarah said, "God has brought me laughter, and everyone who
hears about this will laugh with me." - Genesis 21:5-7

Every week in my Sunday School class, we ask for prayer requests
and share praises. The list for prayer requests is always a lot longer
than our lists of praises. While it is a good thing to ask for others in
Christ to pray with you about your concerns, I also think we should
share what blessings we have received. Someone who is struggling
might need to see what great things God can do!

I assume everyone around Sarah knew she wanted a child. If there
was a prayer request list around her, that would have certainly been
on it. But, she didn't fail to rejoice when Isaac was born. I'm sure she
shared her tears, but also shared her joy and laughter!

Remember today that we need to show those who are lost how
great our God is. My prayer is that everyone who sees me says, "Her
mouth is filled with laughter, Her tongue with songs of joy. The Lord
has done great things for her" (Psalm 126:2)!

_ஒஜ ஜஒ_

October 21

Faith and Trust

Jesus said, "Let the little children come to me, and
do not hinder them, for the kingdom of Heaven
belongs to such as these." - Matthew 19:14

Have you ever watched a child sleep? They can lay their heads down at night and fall asleep easily because they don't worry about tomorrow. Have you ever made a child laugh? It doesn't take much to get a smile from them. Have you ever had a child depend on you? Their trust is instinct. They believe that what they need, you can and will provide. This child-like faith and trust is the kind of faith and trust we should have in Jesus.

Try to fall asleep easily, because you trust in Him. Smile often, because you trust in Him. Believe that He will provide what you need, because you trust in Him. As a child, we had faith and trust in our earthly parents. As adults, let's have that same faith and trust in our Heavenly Father!

ornamental flourish

October 22

Fair Weather Believer

But stretch out your hand and strike everything he has,
and he will surely curse you to your face. - Job 1:11

In the story of Job, Satan is convinced that even true believers are
only faithful as long as life is going well for them. He felt that if all
they held dear was taken away, then they would reject God. "Fair
weather" believers are what he thought we all were. So, the test was
Job.

We learn about suffering from the story of Job. We learn that it is
just a part of life. It often teaches us humility and patience. It shows
us that we are not in control. Through our suffering, we either prove
Satan right or we prove him wrong. Job definitely proved him wrong.
In our suffering, which do we do? Are we fair weather believers?

No More Acting

"These people honor Me with their lips, but their hearts are far from Me." - Mark 7:6

The Scribes and Pharisees of the New Testament had a lot of people fooled. They looked religious. They spoke of religious things. They made grand gestures and followed the laws that were visible. From the outside looking in, they seemed to be pleasing to God. But Jesus saw them from the inside, and He was not fooled.

The Bible tells us, "Man looks at the outward appearance, but the Lord looks at the heart" (1 Samuel 16:7). Acting religious, quoting the Bible, and speaking of Him, won't save you. Letting Him change your heart will save you. Trusting Him. Believing Him. Having faith in Him. These things will save you. And if these things happen in your heart, you won't be "acting" anymore - it will be the real you!

October 24

The Right Road

Narrow is the road that leads to life, only a few find it. - Matthew 7:I4

Did your mother ever ask you, "Well, if your friends jump off a bridge, are you going over with them?" Mine did. I don't remember that statement verbatim, but it's something like that. I don't have kids, but if I ever do, I'm sure my book with all these parental sayings in it will be delivered and I will not get this phrase wrong. I had to be reminded that I don't have to follow the crowd. If only a few find the right road, following the crowd is not a good idea!

Why is it that we don't have to be taught to follow the wrong road? Why is it that we seem to automatically veer off in the wrong direction? Being right and doing right is not always easy and not always our first instinct. There is only one map that leads down the right road and that is God's Word. You will get lost without it!

October 25

This Is It!

Provide yourselves money bags which do not grow old, a treasure in the heavens that does not fail. - Luke 12:33

How many times in your life have you said, "This is it?" There have been times where I thought I was going to get something or achieve something that would make my life perfect. Whether it is a relationship, a job, an investment, a purchase, an event - I have often thought, "If this would just work out, I'd be so happy." This could possibly be true, but even if it works out, the happiness is usually temporary. In this life, people can fail you. Life can disappoint you. Things don't always work out the way you wanted them to.

Building your treasures in heaven is a much safer investment. Building your life around Jesus is not a temporary fix. He is never on shaky ground. His promises will not fail you. He cannot be stolen from you. Nothing can destroy what He builds in you. With Him, your "This is it!" moment will never disappoint and will never end!

Such a Time as This

For if you remain silent at this time, relief and deliverance
for the Jews will arise from another place. - Esther 4:14

In studying Esther, I noticed a part of the story that I had never caught before. When Mordecai was pleading with Esther to go to the king to plead for her people, I got so caught up in whether or not she will die, I didn't catch everything else. Mordecai said "relief and deliverance for the Jews will arise." He had no doubt that God is faithful. He had no doubt that God would not let His chosen people be wiped out. He was basically saying, "Esther, this is going to happen. You just need to decide whether or not you want to be a part of it, or be left out."

God's will is going to happen. We just have to decide whether or not we want to be a part of it. Mordecai never doubted that God would be faithful and save His people. He believed that is why this unlikely girl became the unlikely queen for "such a time as this" (Esther 4:14). What has God set you up for? What is your "such a time as this?" If you need courage, He will be faithful. If you need trust, He will be faithful. If you need grace and mercy, He will be faithful. There is an Esther in all of us. Don't get left out, follow His will!

Energy Booster

Have you not known? Have you not heard? The everlasting God, the Lord, the Creator of the ends of the earth, neither faints nor is weary. His understanding is unsearchable. - Isaiah 40:28

Energy Boosters are the new trend. There are energy drinks, caffeine pills, and many other products on the market today. We sometimes lack the energy to get through the day. Have you ever wondered why this happens? We sometimes forget to take care of ourselves; mind, body, and SPIRIT!

We get tired, frustrated, and weak. This happens. We know it will. We push ourselves to the point of exhaustion. Why? There are different reasons for everyone. It could be ambition. It could be fear of idleness. It could be exceedingly high expectations that we put on ourselves. Whatever our reasons are, God knows our limits. He knows our weakness. He knows our heart.

It's a wonderful thing for us that Our Lord, never "faints nor is weary." It's a blessing to us that Our Lord's "understanding is unsearchable." When we are at our limits, we can be thankful that He has none. His strength comes in our weakness. Because of Him and our faith in Him, He will "renew our strength; and we will mount up with wings like eagles, we will run and not be weary, we will walk and not faint" (Isaiah 40:31). When we look to Him to get us through, He's the best "energy booster" we have!

Natural Disasters

He restores my soul. - Psalm 23:3

In the wake of a hurricane on the coast, tornados tunneling through our state, or earthquakes in California, we always see the aftermath on TV. We see the clean up of debris, the carrying away of trash, and the reconstruction of something new.

Our lives can sometimes seem like natural disasters. A storm can come through and rock our world. People or situations can be like a tornado that leaves a path of destruction. We can even feel like the ground has opened up and we have fallen into a pit of despair holding on to the edge with white knuckles.

No matter what kind of destruction we have in our lives, God can help. He gives us "beauty of ashes, joy for mourning, and a garment of praise for the spirit of heaviness" (Isaiah 61:3). If you seek His help, He comes in to clean up the debris, carry away the trash - "He restores my soul" (Psalm 23:3), and reconstructs something new - "Behold, I make all things new" (Revelation 21:5)!

Christ-Like Qualities

Be kind to one another, tenderhearted, forgiving one another,
even as God in Christ forgave you. - Ephesians 4:32

Who would you rather spend time with, a nice person or a mean person? Who would you want around during a rough time, a compassionate person or someone who could care less? Who seems like a happier person, the one who can forgive or the one who carries around all their bitterness?

I've never regretted saying a kind word to someone, but I have regretted plenty of mean things I have said and done. I never regretted caring for those who needed me, but have regretted those I have left alone in order to seek my own agenda. I have never regretted forgiving someone who hurt me, but have regretted holding on to some bitterness that still seemed to haunt me. Scripture tells us to be kind, tenderhearted, and forgiving because it's what is right, it's what is good. If we seek to have these Christ-like qualities, we will have less in life that gets placed in our "regret" column. These qualities will make life better, for ourselves and for those around us!

ﾟ⊙☙ ☙⊙ﾟ

October 30

A Beautiful Prayer

Search me, O God, and know my heart; test my thoughts.
Point out anything you find in me that makes you sad, and lead
me along the path of everlasting life. - Psalm 139:23-24

I love the verse above. It's just a beautiful, honest prayer. In our daily lives, we are able to fool a lot of people. We might be very nice to someone we don't really like. We might be thinking about how to undermine a co-worker in order to make ourselves look better. We might be getting into relationships that aren't right for us. Still, no one knows and from the outside looking in, all seems right in our world.

In this prayer, the Psalmist asks, "know my heart." Asking God something, He already knows still lets Him know that is what you desire. It's telling Him that even though you have no secrets with Him, it's okay with you that He knows and not just okay, but welcome. "Test my thoughts and point out in me what makes you sad." This, to me, is asking God to make you accountable not only for what you do, but what you think about. It's asking God to be a part of you before you act and in your actions as well. "Lead me along the path of everlasting life." This is asking God to be with you always. And not only to be with you, but to guide you in His way, not yours. Like I said, to me, this is a beautiful and honest prayer. It's like saying, "I know I'm flawed, so I need your help!"

Run for Life

I've already run for dear life, straight to the arms
of God. – Psalm 11:1 (the Message Bible)

In scary movies, the main character spends the whole movie running from something or someone that is trying to kill them. They are always trying to run toward something safe, toward some sort of shelter from harm. Do you ever wonder why they run up the stairs instead of out the front door? Do you ever wonder why they never turn on the lights or always seem to go everywhere alone? Do you ever wonder how they survive making one unwise decision after another?

We are sometimes like this in our Christian lives. Satan is constantly trying to kill us. He's trying to kill our chance for salvation. He's trying to kill our witness and our faith. In these times, we need Jesus! We don't always run in His direction. We don't always use His light to find our way. We often try to handle things on our own. We, at times, make unwise decisions. When we are running for our life, we need to run straight to the arms of Jesus!

November 1

Call Out to Him

If my people who are called by My name will humble themselves, and pray and seek My face, and turn from their wicked ways, then I will hear from heaven, and will forgive their sin and heal their land. – 2 Chronicles 7:14

I think about this verse a lot, especially around election time. During this time, we, as a nation, make huge decisions about our future. We all need to seek God's guidance during times like these. We need to humble ourselves and seek His will, not our own. Seek His truth, not what we think it should be. Seek His way, not the ways of the world.

No matter your politics, seek His guidance and let your voice be heard. If we call out to Him, He will hear us. He will come into our hearts and our lives and our nation!

Harvest Time

Let us not become weary in doing good, for at the proper time
we will reap a harvest if we do not give up. - Galatians 6:9

Sometimes doing the right thing isn't easy. I guess if it was, everyone would do it. Sometimes it's easier to be selfish, to avoid, or take the simple way out. Also, doing the right thing doesn't always make you the popular one. This is why we can't always think of the "here and now" when we are making decisions. We need to think down the road to "harvest time."

Scripture mentions this concept many times. Not everything gets instant rewards, "there is a time for everything and a season for every activity under heaven" (Ecclesiastes 3:1). Not everyone will understand, "The harvest is plentiful but the workers are few" (Matthew 9:37). But the ones who do, "Let us not become weary in doing good, for at the proper time we will reap a harvest if we do not give up!"

November 3

Are You an Example
or an Excuse?

You will follow the example of those who are going to inherit God's promises because of their faith and endurance. - Hebrews 6:12

Our pastor once asked "Are you an example or an excuse?" That question really spoke to me. When a Christian is living outside God's will, they are a huge asset to Satan. What looks worse then a professed child of God living a sinful life? Non-believers will look at them and say, "Why should I go to church? They aren't acting any different than me."

When someone finds out that you are a Christian, they watch and see how you react to certain situations. Do people notice that you go to church every Sunday, but you can tell a dirty joke with enthusiasm? Do they see you sing in the choir, but then get drunk at the company party? Is there anything in you, except church attendance, which sets you apart from a non-believer?

If Jesus lives in your heart, and you are in His will; it will show. You will still be affected when bad times happen, but your reaction should be different. You should show your "Jesus nature" instead of your "human nature." Our behavior may make the difference in someone coming to know Jesus Christ or not.

When I pray daily, I ask that I be an example not an excuse. When people see me, I want them to see Jesus. Ask yourself; are you an example or an excuse?

November 4

Are You Prepared?

No one knows about that day or hour, not even the angels in
Heaven, nor the Son, but only Father. - Matthew 24:36

When the weather reports have predicted a heavy snow, how many
people do you think will go to the grocery store? How many do you
think make sure there was gas in their car? How many will prepare
for the snow, expecting it to come?

It seems scary to me how many people will run around town getting
prepared for a snow storm that may or may not happen, but don't
give a thought about preparing for eternal life. This will happen! We
don't know when and we won't get a news report letting us know this
might be the date. We don't get a day to prepare before hand. Get
prepared today. Come to Jesus and get everything you need!

ᴏᴇ꙰ ꙰ꙺ

November 5

Seeing Not Believing

We live by faith, not by sight. - 2Corinthians 5:7

Have you ever heard someone say, "Well, I'll believe it when I see it?" I've said this myself. When someone says they are going to start exercising regularly, or eating better, or doing anything that we don't believe they will do, we say or think this. It's human instinct to see with our own eyes to order to believe.

In our Faith, the opposite is true. "We live by faith, not by sight." (1 Cor. 5:7) "So we fix our eyes not on what is seen, but on what is unseen. For what is seen is temporary, but what is unseen is eternal." (2 Cor. 4:l8). This concept is hard for some to understand. People are flawed, so with them seeing is believing. God is perfect in every way. He does what He says He will do. He never fails. He is always there. With Him, we don't have to see it to believe it!

November 6

Plank vs. Speck

So the Lord sent Nathan the prophet to tell
David this story....... - 2 Samuel 12:1

In 2 Samuel, God sent Nathan to tell David a story. It was a story about a rich man, who an abundance of sheep and cattle that stole and killed the only lamb of a poor man. As David listened to the story, he grew angry as he heard of this rich man's disregard for something so precious to the poor man. He even said that this rich man deserved to die. He had no clue that Nathan was symbolically talking about him. About how he, who had many wives, had stolen the only wife of a good man. Then, in trying to cover up his sin had that good man killed.

How many of us do this very same thing? The Bible asks us, "Why do you look at the speck in your brother's eye, but do not consider the plank in your own eye?" (Matthew 7:3). We can easily see what someone else is doing as wrong, or how to "fix" their problems. Why can't we see our own as easily? Is it avoidance? Denial? Pride? Selfishness? In my case, it's probably a little of all of these things. I know it's so much easier to pass judgment on someone else's actions, to help figure out what's wrong with "them," and to solve "their" problems. It's easier because it takes the focus off of our wrong actions, our flaws, or our problems. We need to take a look inside today and be more concerned with our "plank" than the "specks" of others!

November 7

Light in the Darkness

Your word is like a lamp for my feet and a
light for my path. - Psalm 119:105

Have you ever been walking in the dark? Whether it's outside with
no street lights, or inside a house with no electricity, it's hard to find
your way without light. If there no way to see where you are going,
you can take a wrong turn, bump into something unseen or fall in a
hole and get hurt. You also could continue in the darkness until you
are so lost that you don't even know where you are anymore. Has
this happened to you? This hasn't only happened to me literally, it's
happened to me spiritually.

We all have dark times in our lives and there is only one way out.
We need to bring Jesus close so His light will shine around us and
study His Word so we will know His path for our lives. He will
keep us from making that wrong turn. He will help us side step
that obstacle. He will help you find our way out of the darkness and
into the light!

November 8

Burning Coals?

If your enemy is hungry, feed him; if he is thirsty, give him something to drink. In doing this, you will heap burning coals on his head. - Romans 12:20

When I read certain verses, I understand what is meant by studying the Bible, rather than just reading it. When I read, "you will heap burning coals on his head," I didn't really think it went well with the previous sentence. If you are supposed to be nice to your enemy, then why would you want burning coals on his head?

In an ancient Egyptian custom, a person who wanted to show public contrition (remorse, repentance) would carry a pan of burning coals on their head. The coals represented the burning pain of shame and guilt. The meaning in the above verse is, if we show kindness to those who haven't been kind in return, it should bring shame to them for their hate and animosity, in other words, we will "heap burning coals on their heads."

We have all heard the saying, "kill them with kindness." I don't think that's necessarily what this means, but it will show that we are different - since it's not human nature to be nice when you don't really want to. As Christians, we are representing our amazing Jesus who showed mercy and kindness to everyone - even those who killed him!

It's All About Him

People may be pure in their own eyes, but the Lord
examines their motives. - Proverbs 16:2

I am blessed to sing with some wonderful ladies in my ensemble group. One, who is a dear friend and spiritual mentor to me, always prays for us before we sing. Her prayer is always the same. She prays that our singing be about His glory, not ours. She prays that His message be heard, not just a pretty song. I'm embarrassed to admit that I used to not think about these things. It was all about how we sounded, what I was wearing, what others thought when they heard me, or was I having a good hair day. I'm sad to admit that "I" was all I thought about. It's also sad to admit that I thought I was ministering to others with an attitude like that.

God knows our hearts, even if we are confused about it ourselves. Glorifying and praising God is what worship is all about. It's not about you! It's all about Him. Our pastor once said, "Don't leave church and ask, "What did I get out of church today?" but ask, "What did I give God today and would it please Him?"

ᴏᴏ ᴏᴏ

November 10

God's Will

No one can know a person's thoughts except that
person's own spirit, and no one can know God's thoughts
except God's own Spirit. - 1 Corinthians 2:11

I sometimes stand in awe of those who seem so in tune with God's will for their lives. I find myself wondering, "How do they do that? When a minister decides to take or leave a church, when a young person decides to dedicate their life to missions, when someone leaves a secure lifestyle to trust God and start a ministry, I sometimes find myself thinking, "How do they just know?" He may want us to share His word with someone from work. He may want us to volunteer somewhere. He may want us to lead a Bible Study or take one. How do we know?

We cannot know God's will unless He is a part of our being, a part of our daily lives, and a part of our daily prayers. I have found that when I keep God close and spend time with Him, I am much more "in tune" with what He wants from me. I'll admit, I sometimes feel like I'm just guessing, but if I am keeping Him close, it's at least an educated guess. We cannot assume we know God's will without seeking guidance from the Holy Spirit. Make seeking Him a part of your day!

※ ※ ※

November 11

Be Silent and Be Still

The eyes of those who see will not be dim, and the
ears of those who hear will listen. - Isaiah 32:3

I read something once that made me laugh out loud. "Never miss a good chance to shut up!" - Will Rogers. This was the exact problem I had been having in my prayer time. I would talk and talk and complain and whine, but after all that I sometimes forgot to be quiet and listen for that "still small voice" (1 Kings 19:12). The Holy Spirit could work in me and through me a lot easier if I would just stop and listen. God had listened to me, after that, it needed to be my turn to "be still and know" (Psalm 46:10).

We are supposed to bring our requests; our hopes, our dreams, and fears to our Father. This is a part of what prayer is, but not all of it. Talk to Him, bring everything about yourself to Him, He wants to hear about it! Then, just be silent and be still with Him and close out everything else. If you do that, it's amazing how your eyes will open and your ears will hear!"

November 12

Opinions vs. Truth

Now this I say lest anyone should deceive you
with persuasive words. – Colossians 2:4

There are many opinions in this world. During this time of year, we are given great examples of this. During elections, we hear that this is what's right or that this is the direction in which our country should go. Turn the channel on your TV and you will hear the exact opposite of what you just heard, but it too is without a doubt the right thing to do. People have strong beliefs and opinions and directions. So, what's right in a world that is so confusing?

What's the truth? Jesus said, "I am the way, the truth, and the life. No one comes to the Father except through Me" (John 14:6). What is right? "Love one another, as I have loved you" (John 13:34). What direction should we be going? "If anyone desires to come after Me, let him deny himself, and take up his cross, and follow Me" (Matthew 16:24). We don't have to be confused by the opinions of this world when we have the truth of the Gospel!

November 13

Tradition vs. Heart

Jesus replied, and why do you break the command of
God for the sake of your tradition? - Matthew 15:3

We had a Sunday school lesson about favoring a tradition or ritual over having a heart for God. Although we don't often compare ourselves to the Scribes and the Pharisees of Biblical times, I think that we should. We need to be careful not to focus so much on what something looks like rather than what something is.

Our world today isn't much different than it was back then. We seem to focus on image, stature, success and power. We seem more concerned about what people wear to church or if the music is too contemporary, than how many people come forward during the invitation. Like the Pharisees, we don't like change even if the change brings more people into a relationship with God. Now we won't admit that is what we think, but our actions show differently. We look sideways at a person that is raising their hands in worship. We act like we don't see a person that doesn't look or dress like we do. We don't support a decision or an idea that is not our own. Sound like the Pharisees to you?

Jesus loved and accepted everyone. He wanted everyone to worship His Father. He wanted everyone to spend an eternity with Him in Heaven. Don't you?

Germ Free

When the Pharisee saw this, he was amazed that He did not
first perform the ritual washing before dinner. - Luke 11:38

Antibacterial gel is a big thing these days. People carry it with them
everywhere. They use it before eating meals in restaurants, douse
their children with it when playing in a public parks; we are obsessed
with whatever pesky germ that might try to jump out and attach
itself to us. The fact is, no matter if you buy this gel in bulk or not,
you cannot escape every germ. Haven't you notice that most cleaning
products advertise that they kill 99.9% of germs. That still leaves
.1%. Point being, we can never be 100% germ free!

The Pharisee in this verse was more concerned with ceremony than
hygiene, I'm sure. But, they were as obsessed with ceremony as we
have gotten with germs. They wanted to look like they were 100%
clean. As we know, this can never happen.

Only through the grace and mercy of Jesus, can we be fully clean.
Not because we washed our hands or performed some ceremonial
rite, but because of Him. His blood is the only cleaner that gets
everything 100% clean!

November 15

Being with Our Father

"Why were you searching for me? He asked. "Didn't you know I had to be in my Father's house?" - Luke 2:49

When Jesus was twelve years old, he traveled with his parents, as he did every year, to Jerusalem for the Feast of the Passover. When the feast was over, his parents headed back to Nazareth and at first they didn't notice that Jesus wasn't with them. Once his absence was realized, they raced back to find him. They were worried, scared and didn't know where he was. Finally, they found him in the temple. When Jesus was asked why he did this, he innocently said, "Didn't you know I had to be in my Father's house?" He knew he wasn't lost; He was just with His Father.

There are times in our lives that we feel lost. We can be confused about where we are going or who we really are. There is no need to be worried or scared. We can find our way home. We can find out Whose we are. One that is lost can always be found. We don't need to be lost; we just need to be with Our Father!

November 16

Hasten Not

The jailer woke up to see the prison doors wide open.
He assumed the prisoners had escaped, so he drew his
sword to kill himself. But Paul shouted to him, "Stop!
Don't kill yourself! We are all here!" - Acts 16:27-28

In this passage in Acts, Paul was in prison. During the night a great earthquake came and shook the prison making the doors fly open and the prisoner's chains fall off. Paul, influenced by the Holy Spirit, knew not to run out into the night to freedom. If he had, the prison guard would have died and instead he came to know Jesus. Since Paul didn't act in haste, one more person will spend eternity with Jesus.

How many times in our own lives to we act in haste? How many times do we think we know what to do, so we don't ask for God's guidance? Since God sent an earthquake to literally "rattle the cage," if I was Paul, I would have gotten out of there! He didn't. His first thought wasn't to save himself, but to do God's will and to save others. If we learn to slow down and not act so quickly, we, like Paul, might have someone come to us and say, "What must I do to be saved?" (Acts 16:30).

Growing Pains

For you know that when your faith is tested, your
endurance has a chance to grow. - James 1:3

Did you have growing pains as a child? I remember one summer, my
legs hurt constantly. I grew several inches in a short period of time.
When I would whine to my mother, she said, "I know it hurts, but
it's just part of growing up." I didn't like the pain, but I certainly
liked being taller. I had always been one of the smallest children
in my class, and now I was able to ride the big rides because I was
no longer below the line!

As you strive to grow in your walk with Christ, you will be tested.
Satan will try and block your path. He will try anything to stunt
your growth. He doesn't have a "no below the belt" rule. I have had
several conversations with friends about "spiritual growing pains."
They can hurt just as much or more than physical growing pains.
But, sometimes we have to hurt to grow. Don't focus on the pain
of growing, cherish the fact that Jesus says, as my mother did, "I
know it hurts, but it's just part of growing up." After your faith has
been tested, and your endurance has grown, you will no longer be
below the line and the big rides won't seem as scary! Don't be afraid
to grow in Him!

ꙮꙮ ꙮ

November 18

Walk in the Light

The light shines in the darkness, but the darkness
has not understood it. - Joh1 1:5

Have you ever wondered why a good idea is often called a "bright idea?" Have you ever wondered why the expression "a light bulb came on" is used when someone finally understands something? When you wake up, what's the first thing you do? Turn on the light! Being in the light is good and understanding and safe. Being in the darkness is confusing and hidden and unsafe.

There are so many references to light and darkness in scripture. Jesus said, "I am the light of the world. He who follows Me shall not walk in darkness, but have the light of life" (John 8:12). "God is light; in Him there is no darkness at all" (1 John 1:5). "If we claim to have fellowship with Him yet walk in darkness, we lie and do not live by the truth" (1 John 1:6). "But whoever hates his brother is in the darkness and walks around in darkness; he does not know where he is going, because the darkness has blinded him" (1 John 2:11). Jesus said in the Sermon on the Mount, "You are the light of the world. A city that is set on a hill cannot be hidden" (Matthew 5:14). And don't forget the first quote from God in all of scripture, "Let there be light"(Genesis 1:3).

There is a reason that a "bright idea" is a good idea. There is a reason a light bulb going off is a good sign. We are to "walk as children of light" (Ephesians 5:8). If not we will be left in darkness and confusion, never understanding how great the light is!

Do You Thank God?

My cup runs over. - Psalm 23:5

I love the 23rd Psalm. Until I spent some time studying it, it was the "Death Psalm" to me. By that I mean, the only time I read it was when it was printed on the program for someone's funeral. In the beautiful words of this passage, David is thanking God for his blessings, his security, his assurance, and most importantly his eternal life.

Do you take the time to thank God for your many blessings? Do you focus on what blessings you have received or what blessing you have not received? Do you remember that if the Lord is your shepherd, you shall not want? I think if you would stop and take an inventory of your blessings, you would, like David, say, "My cup runs over!"

ود&ؤ ؤد،

November 20

Giving Thanks

Thanks be to God for His indescribable gift. - 2 Corinthians 9:15

Every year during this season, we all reflect on what we are thankful for. That list usually includes family and friends, sometimes different hopes and dreams that have come true over the past year.

What do you thank God for? Is it just your list of "worldly wants" that you have received? Do you reflect on what He has done for you? Do you thank Him for the "indescribable gift" of salvation that He gave at such a cost? Thanking God for the things we have in this world is a wonderful thing to do, but remember to thank him for the eternal things He has given you. Those are the most important!

November 21

In Everything Give Thanks

In everything give thanks. - 1 Thessalonians 5:18

It is easy to give thanks sometimes. When a baby is born perfect and healthy, when the job you so desperately wanted is offered to you, when your whole family is home for a holiday - it's easy to thank God for these blessings. What about in other times? The Bible says, "in everything give thanks." Does that mean you need to thank God when a relationship doesn't work out? Yes. God may be saving you from something you can't see down the line. Does that mean you need to thank God when someone else gets picked for an assignment that you really wanted? Yes. God may have been planning something in their life that you can't possibly know about. Does that mean you need to thank God when life disappoints? Yes. God may be preparing you for something you can't understand. In everything give thanks!

We, as Christians, can give thanks in every situation. We can be thankful for the good things because, "every good and perfect gift is from above" (James 1:17). We can be thankful for the unknown blessings because, "No eye has seen, no ear has heard, no mind can conceive the things which God has prepared for those who love Him" (1 Corinthians 2:9). We can even be thankful in difficult situations because, "Blessed is the man who endures temptation; for when he has been approved, he will receive the crown of life which the Lord has promised to those who love Him" (James 1:12).

So, in this season of thanksgiving, in everything give thanks!

Purpose in Prayer

For this reason I kneel before the Father... - Ephesians 3:14

All through the writing of the Apostle Paul, he speaks of what he specifically asks for in prayer. Sometimes for himself, sometimes for others, always for the purpose of God's will and the spreading of His gospel.

I don't know about you, but if I'm not careful, my prayers can become stale, repetitious, or just routine. I need to practice in the imitation of Paul and come to Jesus with specific requests and a heart that my prayers are being heard and have a purpose, that this is my time with my God.

When we pray, we pray for a reason. Is it habit? Is it routine? Is it because you are in a desperate situation and will try anything? Or is it because you truly have faith that Jesus will hear and answer? "For this reason I kneel before the Father _____," you fill in the blank!

His Word is Forever

The grass withers, and the flower drops off, but the
word of the Lord endures forever. - I Peter I:24-25

Have you ever noticed how much our world changes? If you have a cell phone that is more than six months old, you are behind the times. If your clothes are two many seasons old, you are out of style. If you have the same beliefs and morals as those who lived 50 years ago, you are old fashioned. I am so grateful that I have something that never changes in any way. I have God's word!

No matter how the world changes, people change, or I change; I can still go to God's word and it's always true, always up to date, and never has to change to fit the times. If I need faith, I can go to His word. If I need answers, I can go to His word. If I need strength, love, counsel, or hope, I can go to His word. It's there no matter what I need!

November 24

Having Hope

Even when there was no reason for hope,
Abraham kept hoping. - Romans 4:18

How easily do we give up on difficult people or situations? How frustrated do we get when our prayers aren't answered in a timely manner? How long before we start to doubt, get angry, fall into depression, or grow bitter when life isn't going our way? I often pray to have the faith of Abraham. He believed no matter what. He trusted not matter what. He hoped when there was no reason to hope (Romans 4:18).

Jesus said, "Come to me, all you who are weary and burdened, and I will give you rest" (Matthew 11:28). We can come to Jesus with anything. We can trust in His promises. We can remember that through Him, all things are possible. We can have hope, even when the world says there is none!

November 25

Don't Eat the Chips!

Let us hold unswervingly to the hope we profess, for
He who promised is faithful. - Hebrews 10:23

There is a reason that I don't buy potato chips and keep them at
my house. Why? Because I will eat them. The same goes for all
the other junk food that I have grown so fond of over the years. I
know that I can't handle having them around, so there's no point in
testing myself. It would be stupid to buy the chips then sit around
praying, "God, please don't let me eat those chips in my cabinet!"
God gave me wisdom to know that stuff is bad for me (just read the
ingredients). He gave me the plan of how to escape the temptation
(don't buy them). He also gave me mercy when I fail (He will forgive
me if I slip and eat a whole bag!) A silly example may be, but you
get my point.

He give us the tools to avoid temptation, "from infancy you have
known the Holy Scriptures, which are able to make you wise" (2
Timothy 3:15). He gives us the strength to face temptation, "no
temptation has seized you except what is common to man. And God
is faithful; He will not let you be tempted beyond what you can bear.
But when you are tempted, He will also provide a way out so that you
can stand up under it" (1 Corinthians 10:13). And last, even when
we mess up, His mercy still makes us shine because He didn't fail,
"He is able to keep you from falling and to present you before His
glorious presence without fault and with great joy" (Jude 24). With
all of this, we, as Christians, know we can persevere!

November 26

The "What If" Fear

He replied, "You of little faith, why are you
so afraid?" - Matthew 8:26

When my mom has back surgery, I knew it was a simple, routine procedure. But, when we got to talk to her before she was wheeled back to surgery, I left with tears in my eyes. I started thinking things like, "What if she's allergic to the anesthesia they use?" or "What if they drop her in recovery?" or "What if the doctor sneezes right as he starts to cut her open?" Yes, I know, my mind can go just about anywhere!

The disciples were being tossed around in a storm. They were screaming, "Lord, save us! We're going to drown!" Jesus, sleeping soundly in the boat, woke and said, "You of little faith, why are you so afraid?" Then, He got up and rebuked the winds and the waves, and it was completely calm (Matthew 8:25-26). Even in the presence of Jesus, faith can waver.

The disciples thought they were going to drown, but they didn't. I was afraid my mom was going to be one of those 1 in a million bad statistics, but she wasn't. We tend to let the "what if" fear fade our faith. I fight it, but it still seems to happen. I went into that morning before her surgery a proud praying warrior, but at the end of the day, I heard that still, small voice saying, "You of little faith, why were you so afraid?" Is anyone else with me here? Let Him come in. He will rebuke your winds and your waves, and no matter the outcome, leave you completely calm!

The Greatest Blessing

He will be great and will be called the Son of the Most
High. The Lord God will give Him the throne of His father
David, and He will reign over the house of Jacob forever;
and His kingdom will never end. - Luke 1:32-33

At church one night, we sang the hymn, "Count Your Blessings."
I love that song and, of course, it certainly fits this time of year.
I love the fact that right after Thanksgiving, we start celebrating
Christmas. The birth of our Savior, the greatest gift God has ever
given, is that for which I am most thankful. This is a season where
that thankfulness is followed by the focus of His birth and the
celebration of His glory. Could there be any better timing than
that?

During this time, when you are surrounded by family and friends,
while you are eating wonderful food and conversing with those you
love, remember to count your blessings. When I look around and see
what God has given me, you may think it doesn't seem like enough,
but it is. He loves me, and has blessed me, and gave His son for me.
The Greatest Gift has become my Greatest Blessing. Could it get
any better than that?

ᏽᏋ ᏵᏋᏽ

November 28

No Secret Service

Let us then approach the throne of grace with confidence,
so that we may receive mercy and find grace to
help us in our time of need. - Hebrews 4:16

In ancient times, the same as today, rulers were not easily approachable. Usually only their highest advisers could seek their attention. In those times, even wives and family couldn't just go into the presence of their kings without first getting permission. The fact that Jesus was approachable meant something amazing to the ancient believers. Today we would get stopped by the secret service if we tried to get too close to the President. Back then, even trying to enter their courts without permission, could get you killed.

Jesus, the High Priest, makes it easy to come before Him. His grace and mercy is given to us for, not only salvation, but all circumstances life brings. In Biblical times, "grace to you" became a common greeting among believers. They knew what an amazing thing it was to have a King you could approach without worry or fear, and they wanted everyone to have it. There's no secret service with Jesus. No one is going to stop you from coming to Him!

November 29

It's Possible

With God all things are possible. – Matthew 19:26

Have you ever said, "That's impossible!" or "I can't do it?" I have. With my limited human mind and physical ability, some things are impossible for me. But, do you think David could have killed the giant Goliath all by himself with only a sling shot? Do you think Jonah could have survived inside the belly of a fish without divine intervention? Do you think Daniel could have made it through a lions den without a scratch if God hadn't shut the mouths of those blood thirsty animals? These triumphs happened, not because of quick thinking or physical strength or even dumb luck – they happened because of God. With God the impossible becomes possible.

You may think a situation is hopeless. You may think that there is no way you can do something. You may have already accepted defeat. Remember the words of David to Goliath, "You come to me with sword, spear, and javelin, but I come to you in the name of the Lord!" (1 Samuel 17:45) The world can and will come at you with the impossible, but face it in the name of the Lord, with faith and trust in Him, and all things are possible!

Two or Three is Enough!

For where two or three come together in my name,
there am I with them. - Matthew 18:20

Once, I was in charge of getting a group from my church to pray for an event in our city. There was a mix up on days, people were out of town, and I had a family situation going on. I got worried about the amount of people I would have at the prayer tent. Then, I read the above verse.

Jewish tradition required at least ten men (a minyan) to constitute a synagogue or even hold public prayer. This verse tells us that Christ will be with us, even if we are a few short of a required number. What I realized is, two or three hearts that truly want to be there is better than 10 that just fill space. So, I still hoped 100 people would show up to pray, but it's not the ceremonial count that matters, it's the hearts of those who are there, no matter the number!

December 1

Being Content

For I have learned to be content, whatever the
circumstances. - Philippians 4:11

I try not to write devotionals that are all about me, but if you'll forgive me, there is something I feel like sharing. I know many people pick life verses. So often chose are verses of encouragement and strength. On my way to work one morning, I was praying about some stuff that I was struggling with, needing answers for and the above verse (as it usually does when I'm struggling) popped into my head. It has become a part of my request in daily prayer that I learn to be content. This all started after studying this passage in Philippians. I started praying that no matter what is going on around me that my feeling of contentment in Him doesn't change. I started praying that no matter what emotions I might be feeling that my faith in Him doesn't waver.

So, as I was praying one morning, I thought of contentment and just smiled at the thought of Jesus. He is always good, even when life stretches my boundaries. I decided then that this would be a pretty good life verse. Have I finally learned the difference between happiness and joy? Has this prayer request finally been answered? We'll see, as for that day, I was doing pretty well and I praised Him for it!

December 2

The Finisher

Jesus, the author and finisher of our faith, who for the joy that was set before Him endured the cross, despising the shame, and has sat down at the right hand of the throne of God. - Hebrews 12:2

How many of you have started something and never finished? I have. There are half done projects in my house that now just take up space. I assume that one day I might finish what I started, but I've rarely pick old projects back up. I am usually so excited about them in the beginning, but get bored with them and move on to something else.

I love that in this verse where it says Jesus is "the author and finisher of our faith." He came the first time to secure a way to salvation. His battle with death was started, finished, and won. He will come again to take all His children home. "I am the Alpha and the Omega, the Beginning and the End, the First and the Last" (Revelation 22:13). We will not be disappointed in our faith or trust in Him. We won't be stored in the closet and forgotten or cast aside for something new and exciting. He will have the last word, the last stand and the last victory. He will say, "It is finished" again, and as His children, we will be right there with Him!

Rough Waters

Lead me to a rock that is higher than I. - Psalm 61:2

Have you ever been watching a movie and one of the character's gets carried away in rough waters? They are being tossed and turned and beaten down, all the while desperately trying to grab on to something stable, to rescue them from drowning. When that rock or tree limb finally comes along at just the right time, they realize that all is going to be alright.

When we are being tossed to and fro in this crazy world, it's nice to know that we have a rock to grab onto. Jesus has the strength and stability to help us face anything that comes. So, next time you get carried away into rough waters, hold on to Jesus and you will see that all is going to be alright!

Free Gift with Purchase

For it is by grace you have been saved, through faith - and this is not from yourselves, it is the gift of God. - Ephesians 2:8

How many things have we bought in order to get the "free gift with purchase?" I'll admit that I have bought a lot of makeup in order to get a pretty bag full of stuff that I usually never end up using. But, it was free! Not really, I had to spend $21.95 in order to get it and when most things only cost a little less than that, I usually end up having to pick out something else for another $20 in order to get my free gift. I justify it by thinking "Well, I would have bought it eventually anyway." The point is, it cost me something to get my free gift.

This might be why it's hard for us to understand that Jesus isn't a free gift with purchase. He doesn't cost us anything. The cost has already been paid, long ago, on a Roman cross. We've all heard that there's nothing free in this world. In this world, maybe not, because Jesus is not of this world!

For the Lord is Good

For the Lord is good and his love endures forever; his faithfulness
continues through all generations. - Psalm 100:5

When my mom was in the hospital, my dear friend Michael got her a book about answered prayers. It was a collection of several short stories where a prayer had been answered. These sweet stories made me swell with both humility and pride for my amazing Jesus. I got to thinking about the fact that I don't need to read a book in order to fill that way; He has done that much and more for me.

If we all pondered our lives, I would imagine that we could all fill our own book with stories of blessings and answered prayers. As I was thinking about all of this, the above verse came to mind. Remember today that "the Lord is good and His love endures forever; His faithfulness continues through all generations!"

ଈଓ ଓଈ

December 6

Daily Up Keep

I will live with them and walk with them. And I will be their
God, and they will be my people. - 2 Corinthians 6:16

There are times when life seems to get pretty busy. In those times
when every night and weekend can get filled with obligations and just
"stuff" to do. At the ends of the day, I basically come home and go
straight to bed. Because of this, my house can start to look neglected.
The floors need mopping, the surfaces need dusting, and laundry
needs washing. Then when I finally get a break and start the cleaning
up process, it has become an overwhelming job! This is why I try to
do things daily, so it won't get so out of hand.

As Christians, we are individual spiritual houses. Christ lives in us.
If we get too busy to tend to our relationship with Him, things can
get cluttered, our hearts can get dusty, and you're left with a big mess
to clean up. Don't wait until things are so out of hand that it seems
overwhelming. Remember, daily up keep makes all the difference!

ᴏᴉᴇ ᴉᴇᴏ

December 7

Greetings and Salutations

*Grace and peace to you from God our Father and
the Lord Jesus Christ. - 2 Corinthians 1:2*

Do you remember when you were in school and learning how to properly write a letter? I don't remember all the specifics, and if you have ever received a letter from me, you can confirm this point! I do remember learning about the greetings and salutations. I can remember trying to decide whether to start a letter with "dear" or "To Whom It May Concern." I would wonder whether or not to end a letter with "sincerely" or "with best regards." Pretty standard and most of the time, pretty insincere!

The apostle Paul could give us all a lesson in letter writing. He put at the first of his letter to the Corinthians, "Grace and peace to you from God our Father and the Lord Jesus Christ." He ended it with, "May the grace of the Lord Jesus Christ, and the love of God, and the fellowship of the Holy Spirit be with you all" (2 Corinthians 13:14). What better hello and good-bye could you get than that? There was also something else about Paul's greetings and salutations, he truly means the words that he says. Wanting God's grace, love, and peace for the Corinthians wasn't just a way to start and finish a piece of writing, it was the desire of his heart.

First Call

Anyone who is having troubles should pray. - James 5:13

Is there a certain person that you share everything with? When you're upset, who do you call first? When disappointment comes, who do you run to for comfort? When you are scared or confused, who calms you down? Are any of these Jesus?

We have someone who is always available to listen. We have someone who cares about whatever is bothering us. We have someone whose arms are always open to embrace us when we are hurt or scared. That someone is Jesus! Make Him your first call!

A Good Song

For this people's heart has become calloused; they hardly hear with their ears, and they have closed their eyes. Otherwise they might see with their eyes, hear with their ears, understand with their hearts and turn, and I would heal them. - Matthew 13:15

I was listening to a CD a friend made me. I noticed this morning that two of the songs on it, both which I like very much, have different views when it comes to suffering. One is from a Christian artist, the other from the secular genre. I would listen to one and then the other, over and over. The first saying, "When my world is shaking, heaven stands. When my heart is breaking, I never leave Your hands." The second admitting, "I find it kind of funny. I find it kind of sad. The dreams in which I'm dying are the best I've ever had." In the end, I looked into the morning sky, seeing the sun break through the clouds and thanked Jesus for being in my life.

Suffering happens all around us. People get sick, jobs are lost, confusion runs rampant - the difference is Jesus. You can let Him ease your pain just by knowing He is there and no matter what, everything will be alright; or you can suffer in silence and never get any peace. Both stories would make a good song, but only one has a happy ending!

*Lyrics used from "Your Hands" by Katie Herzig, JJ and David Heller, and "Mad World" by Gary Jules.

December 10

The Strongest Metal

*When Joseph woke up, he did as the angel of the Lord
commanded and took Mary as his wife. - Matthew 1:24*

Joseph, a good man of good reputation, was engaged to Mary.
She too, was a good girl of good reputation. All of a sudden, she's
pregnant. Imagine the gossip that flew around Nazareth. Not so
good after all, right? He could have let the pressure to do what
"looks" right over ride doing what "was" right. But, he knew in his
heart that this was the Messiah child. He had the trust and the faith
that what God said was true. Can you imagine what he and Mary
must have gone through?

God doesn't always do things the way we would. Thanks be to him
for that! Also, God doesn't always work in ways that make it the
easiest on us. Just as metal has to be tested to see its strength, so do
we. Mary and Joseph must have been made of the strongest metal,
like titanium. What kind of metal are you? I'll have to admit, I have
aluminum days where I can bend with little effort. Other days, I
may be stronger, like steel, where I have to be beaten and hammered
in order make a dent. And hopefully I have days when God can
look at me, see my faith and trust in Him, and say, "Look, another
titanium!"

Something Great

So was fulfilled what was said through the prophets:
"He will be called a Nazarene." - Matthew 2:23

Some found it hard to believe that Jesus was the Christ, just by the way he came. Bethlehem was a little village, not a big town. Nazareth, where He grew up, wasn't the "in" place to live. Nathanael even said to Philip, "Can anything good come out of Nazareth?" (John 1:46) I guess people expected Him to come in a blaze of glory or from a royal family instead of a poor one. They had expectations of what they assumed He would be. God's plan was a little different. Assumptions and stereotypes left many in unbelief.

We do this today. We sometimes judge what someone is worth by where they are from, by who their family is, by how much education they have, or by how much money they are worth. It doesn't matter to God. God can do amazing things through you, no matter your circumstances. Don't assume you can't do this, or you can't do that. With God all is possible! "Yes, Nathaneal, something great came out of Nazareth!" So, let that Something Great be in you!

༄❀ ❀༄

December 12

The Coming Reign

But you, Bethlehem, in the land of Judah, are by no means
least among the rulers of Judah; for out of you will come a ruler
who will be the shepherd of my people Israel. - Micah 5:2

Do you ever go to work and say, "It's going to rain today?" Why
do you say that? Is it because it looks like rain? Or did you watch
the news that morning and the weatherman told you it was going
to rain? Sometimes both, I know. But, if you say the weatherman,
how does he know this? He knows because he is privy to information
that we are not. That is why you, most of the time, believe what he
predicts.

The prophets were men that God trusted with certain information. It
could be about a certain dark times that were coming. It could be in
the form of a warning to His people. It could be about a deliverance
they had been longing for. Also, it could be about the greatest gift
this world would ever know, the coming Messiah. Isaiah, Daniel,
Zachariah, Jeremiah, Micah, even the Psalms, all told of the coming
Messiah. Every detail, every hope - fulfilled. God left no doubt.
He left no wiggle room. Jesus was the Messiah! Born on that first
Christmas, so long ago.

If you don't really want it to rain, you might choose not to believe
the weatherman. In Christ's day, many didn't want to believe that
Jesus was the Messiah, so they choose to ignore what the prophets
had foretold. In either case, it doesn't/didn't stop either of them from
raining/reigning down!

December 13

God With Us

Now there was a man in Jerusalem called Simeon,
who was righteous and devout. - Luke 2:25

Simeon, an elderly man, had been promised by God that he would
live to see the Messiah. When he saw Jesus, there was no star guiding
the way, there was no angel that came to before explaining the
circumstances in which He would appear. It was the Holy Spirit
that led Simeon to the temple courts where he saw the Child and
knew exactly Who he was. Simeon then took the child in his arms
and praised God, saying, "Sovereign Lord, as You have promised,
you now dismiss your servant in peace. For my eyes have seen your
salvation" (Luke 28:30).

Simeon waited a lifetime to see Someone we have always had. Jesus
came in the flesh to save us and this world. Let the Holy Spirit guide
you like He did with Simeon. Let Him lead you to Jesus. No waiting.
He is here and He is Immanuel, which means "God with us."

おおお おおお

December 14

No Room In the Inn

She gave birth to her firstborn, a son. She wrapped
him in cloths and placed him in a manger, because
there was no room for them in the inn. - Luke 2:7

I love the symbolism of this verse, "there was no room for them in the inn." Even at Jesus' birth, some did not make a place for Him. Through these many years since His birth, some still do not make room for Him. Whether it is career, family, friends, social activities, addictions, money, or other assets and pleasures; we can allow ourselves to be full of everything but Him. He is left no place, no room, both in our lives and in our hearts.

Life gets busy, and certain things, important things, can get crowded out. We will fret about small things, while we ignore the big things. Don't be like this crowded inn many years ago, make room for Jesus. Place Him safely in your heart!

December 15

He is Truth

*The shepherds returned, glorifying and praising God
for all the things they had heard and seen, which
were just as they had been told. - Luke 2:20*

The story of Jesus' birth, the real Christmas story, is not only a wonderful message full of awe and glory, but it also shows that God does what He says. One example in Luke is that the angel appeared to the shepherds and said, "Today in the city of David a Savior has been born to you; He is Christ the Lord. This will be a sign to you. You will find a baby wrapped in cloths and lying in a manger" (Luke 2:11-12). And what did they find? Exactly what the angel had said.

God's Word is truth. There is no doubt about it. You don't have to read it and wonder, is this fact or fiction? The world lies. Even we sometimes lie. But, "God is not the author of confusion, but of peace" (1 Corinthians 14:33). He is truth and love and hope. He sent His son to save the world as these shepherds saw proof of many Christmases ago! In Him, you can trust!

The Most Perfect Gift

But the angel said to them, "Do not be afraid. I bring you good news of great joy that will be for all the people." – Luke 2:10

Have you ever bought someone a gift for Christmas that you just knew was the most perfect gift? Did the anticipation of them opening it on Christmas day have you excited? Then, when they eventually opened it, and they only looked up to say a forced, "thanks," how did you feel? What a blow that is! So much thought and preparation only to be disappointed.

The angel came to deliver good news of a gift that is more glorious than the world had or would ever be given. God gave of Himself to bring us His gift. He gave us His son. Do we look up only to say a forced, "thanks," or do we see His gift, Jesus our Savior, as He truly is, the Most Perfect Gift!

December 17

Tell the World

And this was his message: "After me will come one
more powerful than I, the thongs of whose sandals I am
not worthy to stoop down and untie." - Mark 1:7

It was told in Malachi 3:1 that God would send a messenger before the Messiah and that messenger was John the Baptist. He didn't try to be important or to take the glory for himself. He also didn't stop when it got a little rough. He had a purpose and that is exactly what he did. He "prepared the way" as the prophet had foretold. He told people of repentance, forgiveness and baptism. He told them of the One who was coming.

We, as Christians, all have a purpose. That purpose is to tell people about Jesus. To tell of His forgiveness, salvation and the love and unselfishness that made this salvation possible. We, like John the Baptist, need to "prepare the way" for those who don't know Him!

December 18

He's Right There

The Word became flesh and made His dwelling among us.
We have seen His glory, the glory of the One and Only, who
came from the Father, full of grace and truth. - John 1:14

When I was younger, I would often run to my mother and tell her that I couldn't find something. For example, I might have wanted to wear a certain shirt that day and I couldn't find it in my closet. She would say, "Well, it's in there. You just didn't look hard enough." I, of course, would protest explaining that I did, in fact, look very hard. Soon after this exchange, Mom would go into my closet and within seconds, pull out the very shirt I had just said wasn't there.

Sometimes, what we are looking for is right in front of our face and we still don't see it, because we aren't really looking. We can miss seeing Jesus this way. John 1:10 says, "He was in the world, and though the world was made through Him, the world did not recognize Him." The Jewish people had been seeking and waiting for a Messiah for years. He was right in front of their faces and some still didn't see Him for Who He was. Don't miss what is right in front of you, don't miss seeing Jesus!

ೊ๑ಲ ๑ಲಾ

December 19

For God So Loved the World

For God so loved the world, He gave His only begotten
Son; that whosoever believes in Him will not perish,
but have everlasting life. – John 3:16

I don't know about you, but up until a few years ago, John 3:16 was about the only verse I could quote. A lesson from my childhood and probably the most quoted verse in the Bible. John 3:16, to me, is the true meaning of the Christmas season. Actually, it's the true meaning of every season. Jesus was sent by God, from the beauty and comfort of heaven, to be born in humility, to live in hostility, and to die heinously; all because God loved us. Wow! Can you imagine being loved so much that "He gave His only Son?" I can't.

During this season, don't just remember the Gift God gave to the world, but also remember the sacrifice and love it took to give this Gift in the first place. Remember that God would do anything for you. He has already proven that! Remember this birth long, long ago, and you will truly know the meaning of the Christmas Carol, "Joy to the World, the Lord has come!"

December 20

Purpose to Fulfill

What does "He ascended" mean except that He also
descended to the lower, earthly regions? He who descended
is the very one who ascended higher than all the heavens,
in order to fill the whole universe. – Ephesians 4:9-10

I have a fear of the ocean. This fear is mostly because I have seen all the "Jaws" movies. I don't want to be the unsuspecting dinner to something deadly waiting just under the surface. My oldest niece, Sydnee, loves the water, always has. When she was about two years old, I was watching her splash around in the ocean with her little inflatable tube around her waist. She, being a little bit of a daredevil, went a little too far and a wave came up and turned her upside down, her little feet scrambling in the air. The tube was keeping her from flipping back over and I was the only one around. I couldn't depend on someone else to do what I had to do. I didn't even think. I raced out into the water and flipped her right side up. I went from my comfortable ease to (what I think of) as dangerous surroundings to save her life. When I went into the ocean, I had a purpose to fulfill. When I came out, there was relief that my purpose had been fulfilled. She was crying and scared, but otherwise alright.

After the resurrection, Jesus ascended into heaven's glory having fulfilled His purpose for being born into this earth. Relief must have filled Him as He said, "It is finished." But, as He descended to this earth, as a little baby, He had a purpose – not yet fulfilled. He knew what His life on earth would be like. He knew He would be mocked, persecuted, beaten, and He knew that He would have to die a horrible death. He did what He had to do. No one else could do what He would. So, He came down from comfortable Heaven into dangerous surroundings to save our lives!

Gift Well Spent

On coming to the house, they saw the child with His mother
Mary, and they bowed down and worshipped Him. Then
they opened their treasures and presented Him with gifts
of gold and of incense and of myrrh. – Matthew 2:11

When Jesus was born, the wise men came to worship Him. They not only traveled a long way, but they also carried gifts to present to the Messiah Child. These weren't just any gifts, these were costly gifts. There gifts showed the awe and wonder these wise men felt at meeting Jesus. I'm sure they felt this was money well spent!

This Christmas season, what gifts are you going to give Jesus? Will you give a little of your time? Will you give a little of your money? Will you give some mercy, compassion, or forgiveness to those around you? How much will giving these gifts cost you and will you feel these gifts was money well spent? Jesus' gift to us cost Him His life, I think He's worth it. Don't you?

December 22

Only Human

When the woman saw that the fruit of the tree was good for
food and pleasing to the eye, and also desirable for gaining
wisdom, she took some and ate it. She also gave some to her
husband, who was with her, and he ate it. – Genesis 3:6

Adam and Eve, bless their hearts. They get blamed for a lot, but
we need to remember they were only human. Moses, a great man,
lead our people out of Egypt, by only after killing a man. He too,
was only human. David, where can I start? He was a man after
God's own heart (Acts 13:22), but, he also committed adultery and
orchestrated the death of an innocent man, so he too was only
human. I have been known on occasion to use the "Well, I'm only
human" excuse. Why do we do this? Because it's true.

The human nature of God's people proved the need for a Savior.
God's plan was to save us from ourselves. Jesus was born to be our
Savior and led a sinless life. He died on a cross for sins He didn't
commit. How did He do this? Because He was not human, He was
God!

Nicknames

For unto us a child is born, to us a son is given, and the government will be on his shoulders. And He will be called Wonderful Counselor, Mighty God, Everlasting Father, Prince of Peace. – Isaiah 9:6

Lots of people have nicknames. I have a few friends that if you don't call them by their nickname, no one knows who you are talking about. Sometimes a nickname is a reminder of some past event, or it could be some sort of pet name a family uses that sticks with them. There can also be nicknames that can describe a person more than their given name does.

Jesus had many names. Wonderful Counselor, Mighty God, Everlasting Father, Prince of Peace, Immanuel, Savior – all are names used for Jesus. When you think of Jesus this Christmas season, think of His many names. Think of how they are all descriptions of Who He really is!

December 24

Don't Fear Change

He sent them to Bethlehem and said, "Go and make a careful
search for the child. As soon as you find Him, report to me,
so that I too may go and worship Him." – Matthew 2:8

When King Herod was told of the birth of Jesus, he sent the wise
men to locate Him because feared for his reign. He feared that this
Child would mess up his life. He feared change.

Since the birth of Jesus, some have feared change. Starting with
King Herod, followed by the Pharisees, and still today, there are
people out there that don't want Him messing with their life. They
might fear a loss of power (like King Herod and the Pharisees did).
They might fear a loss of freedom (not realizing that, in sin, we
are never free). They might hear having certain rules to live by or
commandments that are too hard to follow (not remembering "for
God did not send His Son into the world to condemn the world,
but to save it – John 3:17). Fear is one of Satan's greatest tools and
it keeps many from coming to know Jesus. Fear keeps many from
knowing the love and grace and mercy and salvation that knowing
Him brings. Don't fear change. Jesus definitely came to change your
life, but only for the better!

December 25

Merry Christmas!

Glory to God in the highest, and on earth peace,
good will toward men. - Luke 2:14

Jesus came to earth to save the world. That is the reason for the celebration of this season. His wonder and awe and love are never ending. From His birth, to His ministry, to His death, and His resurrection - He did all of this for us!

If you don't think there is anything to celebrate this year, think about Him. If you have more blessings than you could ever count, thank Him. If you have a moment of peace and joy, remember it is from Him. Jesus is the reason for the season and it definitely something to celebrate! Merry Christmas!

December 26

Follow Him

He went out and saw a tax collector named Levi (Matthew),
sitting at the tax office. And He said to him, "Follow Me." So
he left all, rose up, and followed Him. - Luke 5:27-28

I find myself amazed by the first followers of Jesus. He had lots of,
what the secular world, would call "groupies." They followed Him
wherever He went. We, as Christians, know that they were so much
more than that! They abandoned all, not to follow Him around like
those who followed "The Grateful Dead," but because they felt His
call. He didn't say, "Follow Me, I'm the Son of God! With Me you
will be really popular and have riches and see the world!" He just
said, "follow Me" and they just knew. They knew this was a call to
be a part of something bigger than they were. A call to take a leap of
faith that this man had the answers they were searching for. A call
to believe that through Him all was possible.

We might have doubts. We might have things that are just too
precious to us to let go of. We might not have enough faith in
Him and accept that He knows best. Find the faith of those early
believers, rise up, and follow Him!

December 27

Joy Expressed

But the father said to his servants, "Quick! Bring
the best robe and put it on him. Put a ring on his
finger and sandals on his feet." - Luke 15:22

In the Parable of the Prodigal Son (Luke 15:11-32), the rebellious son finally comes home to his father and without a single word of scolding, the father shows and shares his joy. He gave him a robe, which in Jewish custom was reserved for the guest of honor. He gave him a ring, which also was Jewish custom as a symbol of authority. And last, he put sandals on his feet. This showed his membership in the family. This son had only asked to be a slave to his father. He didn't feel he deserved that, but definitely no more than that. In this time, slaves rarely wore sandals.

Even when we have messed up big time, our Father is always ready to welcome us home. He will put a robe across our shoulders, a ring on our finger, and sandals on our feet. We are no longer a slave to this world, because we are His!

In My Heart

Now faith is being sure of what we hope for and
certain of what we do not see. - Hebrews 11:1

This verse is written in a form of Hebrew poetry. The Psalmists often used it. Two combined statements coming together to state the same thought. "Now faith is being sure of what we hope for" - This is the God-given assurance of a future promise. "Certain of what we do not see" - Genuine faith is not based on evidence, but on a belief in Him.

I have trouble explaining faith to a non-believer. It's not something I can show them, as I can the sun or a tree. Of course, they should be able to tell that I'm different. I should show mercy, compassion, gentleness, love, etc. But, my faith is something I feel in my heart. I have often wished that I could allow someone to see inside my heart. Then, there would be no problem. They could see that I am sure of what I hope for and certain of what I do not see!

Jesus' Team

When the net was full, they dragged it up onto the shore, sat down, and sorted the good fish into crates, but threw the bad ones away. That is the way it will be at the end of the world. - Matthew 13:48-49

Do you remember when you were little, about to play a game, and the "self-appointed" captains were picking teams? Didn't you always want to be picked (and hopefully not last!)? No one likes to be left out of the game. In the end, if you weren't picked, often the people choosing would act like they didn't know you or didn't see you. I guess you can see that this has happened to me.

Anyone can play on Jesus' team. You don't have to have great skill, great intelligence or great ability. The only thing required is willingness. The willingness to accept Him as your Savior and Lord.

When Jesus returns, He will be taking His children home. He will be sorting out those who are His and those who aren't. In the end, if you aren't picked, you will hear Him say, "I never knew you!" (Matthew 7:23) Don't let this happen to you!

I Stand in Awe

Then the Lord said: "I am making a covenant with you. Before all your people I will do wonders never before done in any nation in the entire world. The people you live among will see how awesome is the work that I, the Lord, will do for you." - Exodus 34:10

Once, I heard some amazing news that I had prayed for. I knew that God, if it was His will, could and possibly would answer this prayer. When I see a prayer get answered, I stand in amazement of my Savior Lord. I love music and worship a lot through music, so when I heard this news, I caught myself immediately singing the song, "I Stand in Awe of You." If you know this song, you will probably have it stuck in your head the rest of the day. Oh well, good - it's a great song!

I have been taught once again that I have an amazing and awesome God that truly can take my breath away. There are many times that this world can and will let us down, but He never does. He is faithful, hears our prayers, wipes away our tears and brings us strength, peace and comfort. He "does wonders never before done in any nation in the entire world!"

If you pay attention to the world around you, you can always find something to thank God for and to praise God for. There is always a reason to "stand in awe" of Him! Look around and sing it with me!

Being Grateful

In everything give thanks. - 1 Thessalonians 5:18

Tomorrow starts a new year and a lot of people will be thinking about making their "new year's resolutions." I have never been very good at keeping New Year's resolutions, so I stopped making them year's ago. I think this year I will start again. This year I want to be more grateful!

When a year ends, some tend to think about what in the past they didn't get that they really wanted. Others will think of past failures that they want to change. Even others will think, "Well, last year stunk, so this year probably will too!" Why is the tendency to focus on those blessings we didn't get, rather than those we did?

I encourage you to join me in my resolution to be grateful. I want to focus daily on what God has done for me. A grateful heart finds it hard to regret, to be negative, or to fall into self-pity. I bet we would find it really hard to complain and be grateful at the same time! "Be joyful, pray without ceasing, and in everything give thanks, this is the will of God for you life" (1 Thessalonians 5:16-18). Being is grateful is part of doing God's will. Make a resolution to do that!